changes

ENGLISH FOR INTERNATIONAL COMMUNICATION

1
WORKBOOK

Jack C. Richards

with Jonathan Hull
and Susan Proctor

CAMBRIDGE
UNIVERSITY PRESS

PUBLISHED BY THE PRESS SYNDICATE OF THE UNIVERSITY OF CAMBRIDGE
The Pitt Building, Trumpington Street, Cambridge, United Kingdom

CAMBRIDGE UNIVERSITY PRESS
The Edinburgh Building, Cambridge CB2 2RU, UK
40 West 20th Street, New York, NY 10011–4211, USA
477 Williamstown Road, Port Melbourne, VIC 3207, Australia
Ruiz de Alarcón 13, 28014 Madrid, Spain
Dock House, The Waterfront, Cape Town 8001, South Africa

http://www.cambridge.org

First published 1994
Seventh printing 2001

Printed in the United Kingdom at the University Press, Cambridge

ISBN 0 521 44798 4 Student's Book 1
ISBN 0 521 44935 9 Teacher's Book 1
ISBN 0 521 44932 4 Workbook 1
ISBN 0 521 44941 3 Class Cassette Set 1
ISBN 0 521 44938 3 Student Cassette 1

Contents

Please call me Jill

1 **Write about yourself.**

My first name is ....

My last name is ....

Please call me ....

I am from .... (city).

I am .... (nationality).

I am a/an .... (job).

2 *Names*

Tick (✔) the correct forms and cross (✘) the incorrect ones.

a Hello. I'm Walker. ....   d Hello, Mr Pierre Dupont. ....

b My name is Pierre Dupont. ....   e I am Margaret Jenkins. ....

c Hi, Mr Pierre! ....   f Hello, Ms Jenkins. ....

Match the following.

a a full name with a title   1 .... Peter

b a first (given) name   2 .... Ms

c a full name without a title   3 .... Ms Valeria Carletti

d a family name (surname)   4 .... Jean-Pierre Lafon

e a title for a woman   5 .... Vanek

3 **Complete the conversation with the words below.**

a   am   from   is   what   Where   come

A: Hi! I .... Nikos.

     What .... your name?

B: I .... Janice.

A: And .... is your last name?

B: My last name .... Lane.

A: Are you .... England, Janice?

B: No, I .... from New Zealand.

A: Oh? .... in New Zealand?

B: I .... from Wellington.

     I'm a reporter. How about you?

A: I'm .... teacher.

4 **Put the sentences in the correct order to make a conversation.**

.... I'm from Stirling in Scotland. I'm a student.
Are you a student, too?

.... I'm Juliet Roxas. Pleased to meet you.

.... No, I'm not. I'm a sales representative.

.... Pleased to meet you, too.
Where are you from, Juliet?

.... Hello. I'm James Anderson.

.... The Philippines. How about you?

5 **Find the names of three jobs and four countries.**

a cayrseetr   secretary ....

b ecetahr   t ....

c arganem   m ....

d otdrco   d ....

e glumieb   B ....

f pisan   S ....

g cxemio   M ....

h rkyeut   T ....

6 **Look at the answers. What are the questions?**

a What ....?
My first name's Giorgio.

b What ....?
My last name's Vigano.

c Are .... architect?
No, I'm not.

d What ....?
I'm an engineer.

e Where ....?
Venice.

7 **Complete the sentences.**

a They're my classmates. .... names are Julie and Hans.

b We study English. .... class is number nine.

c That's Mr Ono. .... is in my class.

d Please call .... Carmen.

e That's .... teacher. .... name is Ms King.

8   **Where are these countries?**

Write **A** for Asia, **AF** for Africa, **E** for Europe, **ME** for Middle East, and **SA** for South America. More than one answer is possible. Use a dictionary to help you if necessary.

.... Brazil   .... France   .... Kenya   .... Peru

.... Taiwan   .... Chile   .... Italy   .... Korea

.... Portugal   .... Turkey   .... China   .... Japan

.... Kuwait   .... Saudi Arabia   .... Uruguay   .... Egypt

.... Jordan

.... Nigeria

.... Spain

.... Poland

What is the nationality for each country?

Example
Brazil – Brazilian

9   **Look at the answers. What are the questions?**

a Are ....?
    No, I'm not. I'm a teacher here.

b Are ....?
    No, I'm not from Mexico. I'm from Brazil.

c Is ....?
    No, my teacher isn't from Oxford. She's from Glasgow.

d What ....?
    Their names are Sarah and Karen.

e Is ....?
    Yes, she's Japanese.

f I'm Chinese. How ....?
    I'm French.

10 **Choose the correct response.**

a Hello.

.... Hello.

.... See you later.

b Have a nice weekend.

.... Yes, it is.

.... Thank you. And you.

c Excuse me. Are you from Sweden?

.... Yes, he is.

.... No, I'm not.

d See you on Saturday.

.... Yeah, bye.

.... Yes, I am.

e By the way, are you on holiday?

.... No, I'm not.

.... I'm a teacher.

11 **Rewrite the sentences. Use the words in brackets.**

Example
I'm George de Souza. (name)
My name is George de Souza.

a I'm from Canada. (come)

....

b I'm an architect. And you? (How...?)

....

c She is a reporter and he is a reporter. (reporters)

....

d She is Turkish. (Turkey)

....

e You are a student and I am a student. (students)

....

12 **Translate these sentences into your language. Use a dictionary or work with someone who speaks your language.**

a Where do you come from? ....

b What are their names? ....

c Please call me Katherine. ....

d Bye! See you on Thursday. ....

e By the way, my name's Marc. ....

f Have a nice weekend. ....

13 Rewrite these sentences with contracted forms.

Example
He is a student.
He's a student.

a Where is she from?

....

b She is Mexican.

....

c What is your name?

....

d They are classmates.

....

e I am not French.

....

14 Read the text below and answer the questions.

Christos is an English student. He is from Thessaloniki in Greece. Elena de Jong is in his class. She is a reporter. She is Dutch and she is from Nijmegen. Their teacher is from Cambridge. His name is John Peters.

a Are Christos and Elena English students?

....

b Where is their teacher from?

....

c Is Christos from Piraeus?

....

d Is Elena a lawyer?

....

e Is she from Holland?

....

2 It's a great job!

1 **Read the personal profiles and find the correct job.**

photographer   actor   sales assistant   factory worker   cook   architect
scientist   mechanic   journalist

a I work for a food company. I pack food in boxes.

   ....

b I work for a newspaper. I take pictures of people in the news.

   ....

c I work for a garage. I repair cars.

   ....

d I work in a department store. I sell jewellery.

   ....

2 *Pronunciation*

Underline the stressed syllable in each word.

after<u>noon</u>   hotel   photographer   restaurant   department   Japanese
receptionist   university   tomorrow   cleaner   interesting   mechanic
secretary   manager   Wednesday

3 Complete this conversation.

A: What ....?

B: I teach English to foreign students.

A: Really? Where ....?

B: In a language school in Cambridge.

A: That .... interesting.

B: Yes, it's .... ! I love it!

And what ....?

A: I'm an engineering student ....university.

And I .... a part-time job in a department store.

B: Really? What ....?

A: I sell cameras. Do you want to buy one?

4 *What a job!*

The article *a* or *an* is missing from each sentence in these descriptions. Write *a* or *an* in the correct place.

a I'm ⟨ᵃ driver. I work for travel company. I drive bus, and I take people on tours.

b I'm nurse. I work in hospital. I have interesting job.

c I'm waitress. I work in Italian restaurant. I'm also part-time English student at night school.

d I'm teacher. I work in primary school. It's great job.

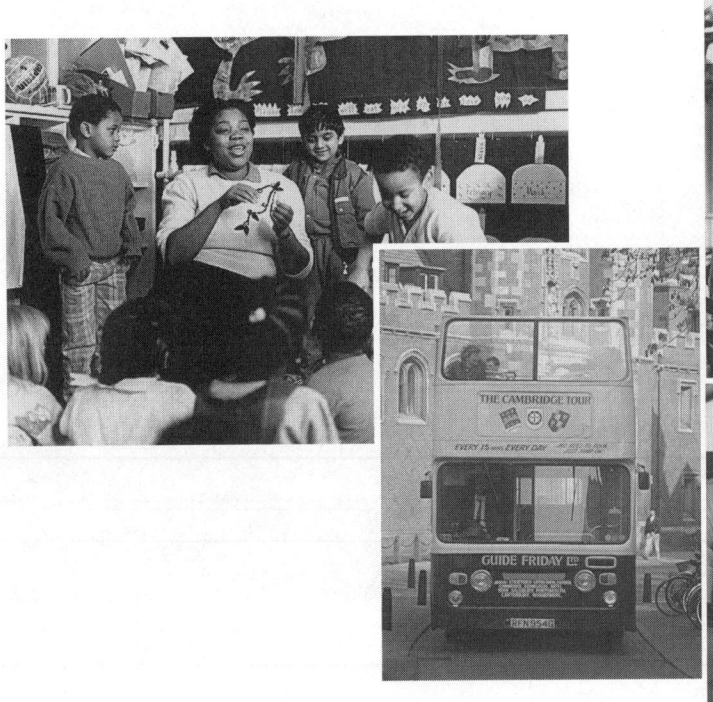

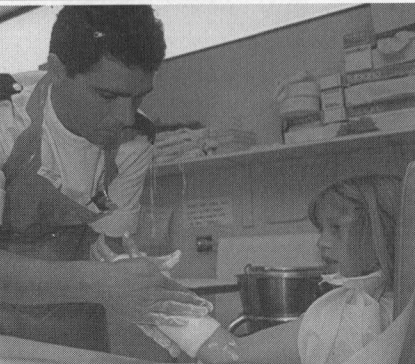

What do you do? Now write about yourself.

....

....

5 Match the work places with the job. Then write sentences.

Example
I work in a restaurant. I'm a waiter.

1	restaurant	a	bank clerk ....
2	office	b	actor ....
3	hospital	c	sales assistant ....
4	garage	d	mechanic ....
5	shop	e	supervisor ....
6	hotel	f	teacher ....
7	school	g	receptionist ....
8	bank	h	nurse ....
9	factory	i	secretary ....
10	film studio	j	waiter ....

....

....

....

....

....

....

....

....

....

6 Choose the correct preposition.

a A: Do you work .... (for/to) a bus company?

B: No. I work .... (to/at) IBM now.

I work .... (from/in) the sales department.

b A: I hate my job! I work .... (for/at) a publishing

company. I'm .... (in/for) the accounts

department. It's really boring. How about you?

B: I love my job. I work .... (from/in)

the Ritzy Hotel. I'm a receptionist there.

c A: Do you work .... (in/to) a school?

B: No, I work .... (from/at) a university. I teach

.... (in/from) the languages department.

I teach Spanish.

d A: Where do you study?

B: .... (For/At) the university. I'm ....

(in/on) the engineering department.

7   Choose the correct response.

a Thank you very much.   .... You're welcome.

                               .... That's right.

b How are you doing?   .... Fine, thanks.

                               .... Yes, it is, thanks.

c I work for a film company.   .... It's a great job.

                               .... That sounds interesting.

d I work in Japan now.   .... Oh, are you?

                               .... Oh, really?

e Is your phone number 874 3215? .... That's right.

                               .... No, thanks.

8   *Crossword puzzle: Verbs*

Use these verbs to complete the crossword puzzle.

repair   love   teach   answer   do   work   take   serve   sell

Across clues

1 I .... French to students at university.

4 Where do you ....? In a night club. I'm a DJ.

5 I'm a sales assistant. I .... cameras and TVs.

7 We're mechanics. We .... cars.

8 It's a great job. I .... it!

Down clues

1 I'm a bus driver. I .... people on tours.

2 I'm a receptionist. I .... the phone and greet people.

3 What do you ....? I'm an architect.

6 Flight attendants .... passengers on planes.

9   Fill in the missing words in the job adverts below.

Waiter   afternoons   Call   good   Part-time   company   full-time   nurses
write

London hospital needs

....

Work ....

or part-time. Call 874

5619 or .... to

Box 361.

.... for
Mexican restaurant.
Work ....
and evenings.

....

El Passo restaurant
on 8729135.

.... job for
language student. Mornings
only. Sell advertisements for
telephone ....
Need ....
English and French.
Write Box 3224.

10 Rewrite the sentences. Use the words in brackets.

Example
I drive trains. (I'm)
I'm a train driver.

a I'm very well, thanks. (fine)

....

b What's your job? (do)

....

c I'm a bank clerk. (work for)

....

d What a great job! (sounds)

....

e It's a good job. (not/bad)

....

f I work in the mornings, not the afternoons. (part-time)

....

11 Translate these sentences into your language. Use a dictionary or work with someone who speaks your language.

a What do you do?...

b She has a part-time job...

c That sounds interesting!...

d Where do you work?...

e How are you doing?..

f What's your address?..

12 Put the following sentences in the correct order to make a conversation.

a OK. Good. And what's your passport number, please? ....

b Is that Berry with a 'y'? ....

c Martin Berri. ....

d And your address, please? ....

e No, with an 'i'. ....

f What's your name, please? ......1.......

g 18 avenue Friedland, Paris. ....

h You're welcome. ....

i Thank you. ....

j 5329618J. ....

I'm just looking, thanks

1 How much is it?

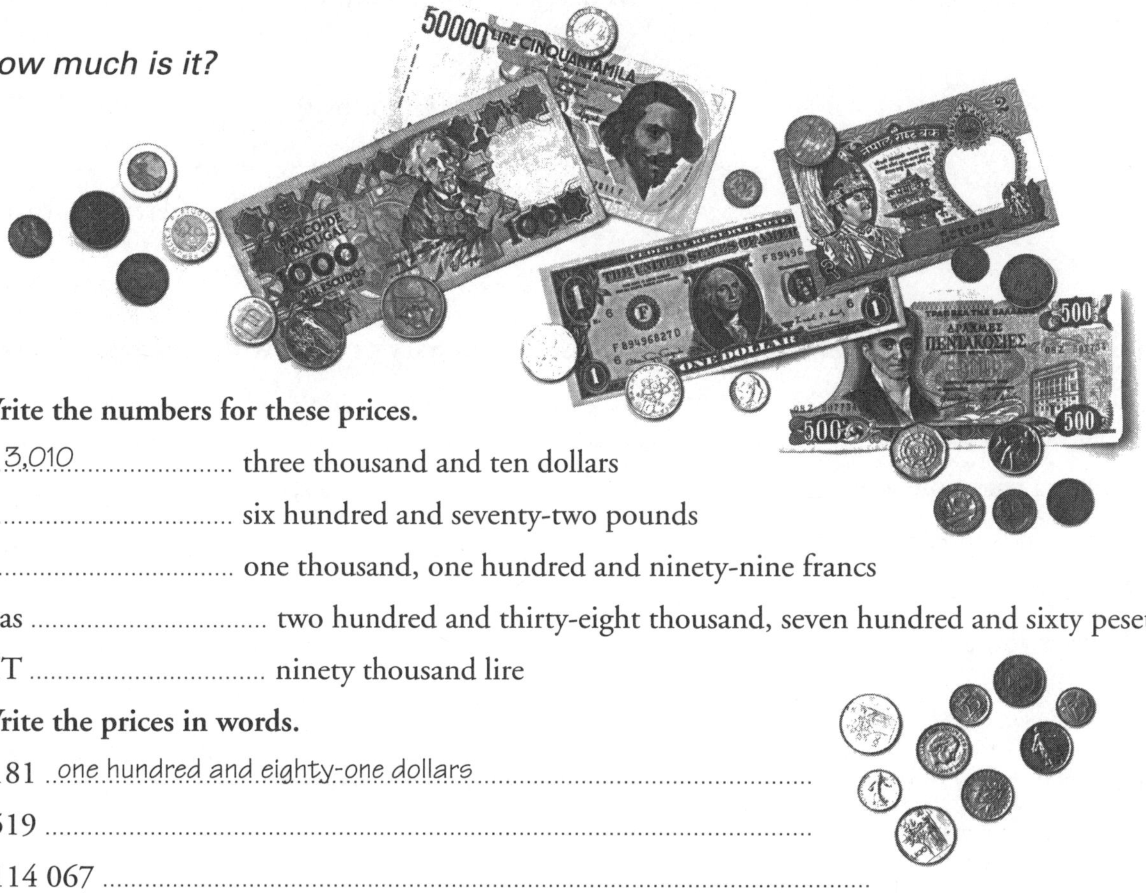

Write the numbers for these prices.

$ .3,010........................ three thousand and ten dollars

£ .... six hundred and seventy-two pounds

F .... one thousand, one hundred and ninety-nine francs

Ptas .... two hundred and thirty-eight thousand, seven hundred and sixty pesetas

LIT .... ninety thousand lire

Write the prices in words.

$181 .one hundred and eighty-one dollars..

£519 ....

F114 067 ....

Ptas 1 089 ....

LIT 24 200 ....

2 Expenses

How much do these things cost in your city?

An English language text book costs about ....

A telephone call is ....

A good pair of jeans costs ....

Now write about the cost of five other things in your city.

....

....

....

....

....

3 **Circle the word that does not belong in each list.**

a (bracelet)   jacket   trousers   shirt

b motorbike   bus   car   road

c bookcase   briefcase   sofa   dining table

d calculator   computer   pencil   typewriter

4 **Circle the correct pronoun.**

A: Amanda, are these socks (your/yours)?

B: No, those aren't (my/mine). (My/Mine) socks are red!

A: I think this is (Linda's/Linda) new racquet.

B: No, that's not (her/hers).

A: Are these Rachel's and Miriam's shoes?

B: Yes, they're (their/theirs).

A: And are these (your/yours) bags?

B: No, sorry. They're not (our/ours).

5 *Spelling check*

Plural nouns	
Add -s	bag — bags
Drop y and add -ies	factory — factories
Add -s or -es	college — colleges
	glass — glasses

Write the plurals of these words.

a bank .....banks.....   e briefcase ....   i shirt ....

b bus ....   f dress ....   j shoe ....

c city ....   g office ....   k dishwasher ....

d company ....   h secretary ....   l actress ....

6 Pronunciation

Put the plural nouns in Exercise 5 in three lists.

Words ending with /z/	*Words ending with* /s/	*Words ending with* /ɪz/
....	.....banks.....................	....
....	....	....
....	....	....
....	....	....
....	....	....

7 Circle the correct pronoun.

A: Good afternoon. Can I help you?
B: Yes. How much is (this/these) necklace?
A: It's £99.
B: Oh. How much is (that/those) one?
A: (It's/They're) only £40.
B: Oh, well. Thanks anyway.

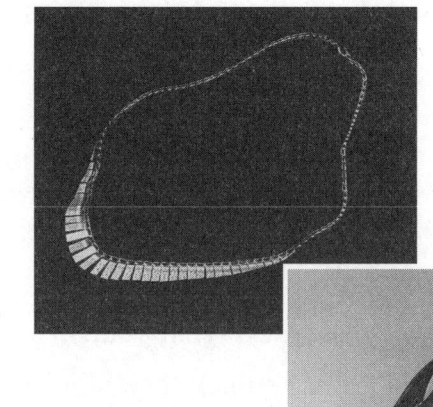

A: Excuse me. How much are (that/those) shoes?
B: (It's/They're) 110 000 lire.
A: Well, I'm just looking, thanks.

A: Are (this/these) stereos in the sale?
B: No, (it/they) are not.
A: How much is (this/these) Sony?
B: (It's/They're) £195.95.
A: And how much are (that/these) headphones?
B: (It's/They're) only £35 each.
A: Oh, really? Thanks.

8 *For sale!*

Write descriptions of these four things.

bicycle for sale   I have a bicycle for sale. It's a Raleigh.
Raleigh   It's two years old. I want £50 for it.
2 years old
£50

a colour TV for sale   c two stereo speakers for sale
   6 months old   £150   2 years old   £75

   ....
   ....
   ....

b camera for sale   d car for sale
   Kodak   4 years old   £25   Volkswagen   20 years old   £400

   ....
   ....
   ....

Now write descriptions for two things you want to sell.

....
....
....
....

9 Look at the pictures. What are the people saying? Match the sentences with the pictures.

a How much is that bag?   It's £26.

b Is that racquet in the sale?   Sorry, it's not.

c Is this your racquet?   Yes, it's mine.

d Is this her bag?   No, it's not.

e How old is that car?   It's two years old.

f What model is this car?   It's a Fiat.

1 ....

2 ....

3 ....

4 ....

5 ....

6 ....

10 Match the advertisements with the pictures.

c

for cooks who don't like to clean:

the ACH984 Cooker

✦✦✦✦✦ Electric oven and hob ✦✦✦✦✦

✦✦✦ Stay clean oven linings ✦✦✦✦

✦✦✦ Interior light ✦✦✦

✦ White or brown colour choice ✦

Pearl

A practical, attractive phone with:

★ 100 name and number memory

★★ Pocket size format

★★★ Attractive grey styling

★★★ Large button format

★★★★★ Volume control

★★★★★★ Battery level display

★★★★★★★ only £299

a

b

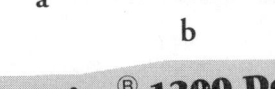

Aquarius® 1200 Delux 9546

Washing machine

❖❖❖ Up to 5kg dry weight capacity ❖❖❖

❖❖❖ 33 Programme Combinations ❖❖❖

❖❖❖❖❖ Lockable door ❖❖❖❖❖

❖❖ 'No Heat' Economy Wash Button ❖❖

Washes *all* your clothes well!

1 ....

3 ....

2 ....

11 Rewrite the sentences. Use the words in brackets.

Example
How much does it cost to go to the cinema? (How much is ...)
How much is the cinema?

a What are your monthly expenses on food? (spend on)

....

b The price of the ticket is £10.99. (cost)

....

c That's not our car. It's their car. (theirs)

....

d Is there a reduction on these calculators? (in the sale)

....

e What's the price of the racquets? (How much/those)

....

f How much do you want for your car? (price)

....

g The pens are Bill's and Ann's. (They/theirs)

....

12 Translate these sentences into your language. Use a dictionary or work with someone who speaks your language.

a We're just looking, thanks.

....

b I spend £50 a month on food.

....

c Those shoes are yours, not mine.

....

d Is that bracelet in the sale?

....

e How much is it, please?

....

f Is it still for sale?

....

g Can I come and see it?

....

h Let me see.

....

What kind of music do you like?

1 **Answer the questions. Use the expressions below and the correct pronouns.**

Do you like ... ?	Yes, I do.	I like ..... a lot.
		I quite like ....
	No, I don't.	I don't like ..... .
		I can't stand ..... .

a Do you like jazz? Yes, I do. I like it a lot. ....

b Do you like horror films? ....

c Do you like Prince? ....

d Do you like classical music? ....

e Do you like opera? ....

f Do you like Madonna? ....

g Do you like rock music? ....

h Do you like TV game shows? ....

2 *At the cinema*

Look at the pictures from five films. What kind of films are they? Choose from the words below.

western   horror   thriller   science fiction   comedy

1 ....   2 ....

3 ....

4 ....   5 ....

3 Write answers to the questions.

a Who is your favourite film star? ....

b What is your favourite kind of music? ....

c Do you like the news? ....

d Does your friend like the same music as you? ....

e What do you think of classical music? ....

f How much TV do you watch a week? ....

4 Choose the correct response in B for each sentence in A.

A

a Would you like to see a film tonight?

b Do you like folk music?

c There's a football match tonight.

d What do you think of Tina Turner?

B

.... I can't stand them.

.... I can't stand it.

.... She's great!

.... How about you?

.... Yes, that sounds good.

.... Great, let's go!

.... I don't agree.

5 Complete the conversation with the correct preposition; *at* or *on*.

A: Would you like to go to the theatre, Liz?

B: Yes, that sounds good. When?

A: There's a comedy .... the Playhouse .... Wednesday.

B: Really? What's it called?

A: It Runs in the Family. It's a new play.

B: Great. OK. The Playhouse .... Wednesday. What time?

A: It starts .... 8 o'clock, so let's meet .... 7.30.

B: OK. How about .... the town hall?

A: Fine, so see you .... the town hall, ... Wednesday .... 7.30.

6 Write questions using the words in brackets. Then match your questions to the correct answers.

a (you/like/rock music) ....

b (she/like/nature programmes) ....

c (you/watch/TV/lot) ....

d (What/favourite/band) ....

e (fancy/concert) ....

f (Where/concert) ....

g (What time/ film/start) ....

.... At the college.   .... Yes, that sounds great.   .... Yes, I do.
.... The Rolling Stones.   .... No, she can't stand them.
.... No, I don't.   .... At 8 o'clock.

7 Write about the films at the Film Festival.

International Film Festival

APOLLO
Friday, July 22
French film:
A Man and a Woman
6.00 pm
Chinese film:
Shanghai Story
8.00 pm

ABC
Saturday, July 23
Canadian film:
Love in Winter
6.30 pm
Japanese film:
Autumn Colours
8.15 pm

CURZON
Sunday, July 24
American film:
Star Wars
5.45 pm
Brazilian film:
Black Orpheus
7.00 pm

There's a French film at the Apollo on Friday, July 22nd at 6 o'clock.

The film is called A Man and a Woman.

....

....

....

....

....

....

....

....

....

....

....

....

....

8 **Use the words in brackets and make questions to ask:**

  – who her favourite singer is. (Who ...) ......Who is her favourite singer? ....

  – when the film starts. (What time ...) ....

  – if I like heavy metal. (Do ...) ....

  – if Jamie watches a lot of TV. (Does ...) ....

  – where the art exhibition is. (Where ...) ....

  – if I want to go to the theatre. (Would ...) ....

9 **Circle the word that does not belong in each list.**

a horror film   western   thriller   (folk)

b jazz   classical   news   rap   heavy metal

c nature   singer   sport   game show   soap opera

d a lot   very much   really   great

10 *Crossword puzzle: That's entertainment!*

Across clues
3 ET is my favourite ... fiction film.
6 Meryl Streep is a very good ... .
8 Do you like to watch soap ... ? No, I don't
   think they're interesting.
9 There's a football ... in the park at 3 o'clock.

Down clues
1 Let's go to the ... to see a play.
2 TV brings ... from around the world into
   people's homes.
4 I really love ... music; Mozart is my favourite.
5 I want to go to the ... to see a film.
7 Gloria Estefan is my favourite ... .

11 **Rewrite the sentences. Use the words in brackets.**

Example
Do you like jazz? (think of)
What do you think of jazz?

a Classical music is OK. (quite like)

....

b I think horror films are great! (love)

....

c He loves sports programmes. (crazy about)

....

d I don't like them! (stand)

....

e Would you like to go to a football match? (fancy)

....

12 **Translate these sentences into your language. Use a dictionary or work with someone who speaks your language.**

a Sounds like a good idea.

....

b I can't stand sport!

....

c There's a science fiction film at the cinema at 7 o'clock.

....

d I really don't like them. Do you?

....

e Do you like her? Not much.

....

13 **Put the sentences in the correct order to make a conversation.**

B: 10 o'clock. ....

A: Where is the display? ....

B: What? ....

A: No, I can't stand them. ....

A: Do you like them? ....

A: What time do the fireworks start? 1

B: It's in the park. ....

B: Yes, I do. Do you? ....

A: Fireworks. ....

How many people are there in your family?

1 Family tree

Look at the family tree and complete the sentences. Then write your own sentences about the family.

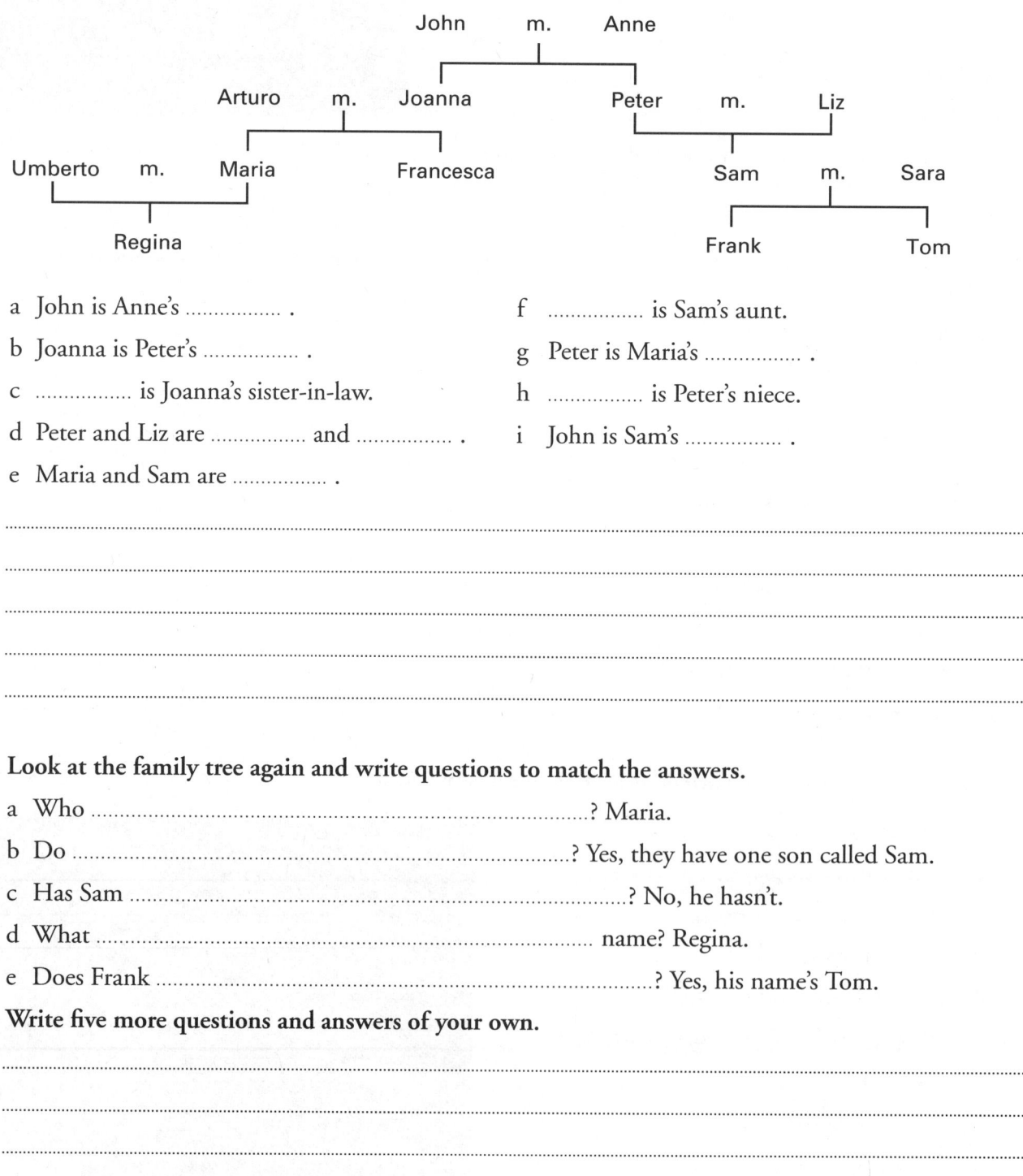

a John is Anne's ....

b Joanna is Peter's ....

c .... is Joanna's sister-in-law.

d Peter and Liz are .... and ....

e Maria and Sam are ....

f .... is Sam's aunt.

g Peter is Maria's ....

h .... is Peter's niece.

i John is Sam's ....

....

....

....

....

2 Look at the family tree again and write questions to match the answers.

a Who ....? Maria.

b Do ....? Yes, they have one son called Sam.

c Has Sam ....? No, he hasn't.

d What .... name? Regina.

e Does Frank ....? Yes, his name's Tom.

Write five more questions and answers of your own.

....

....

....

....

3 Write questions using the words below.

Example
(How many / family)
How many people are there in your family?

a (Have / got / brothers and sisters) ....

b (What / brother / do) ....

c (your grandfather work) ....

d (How many children / have) ....

e (you married) ....

f (your daughter / go / school) ....

g (your children / live with you) ....

h (What / your mother's name) ....

i (Where / your father work) ....

j (Has your grandmother / a job) ....

Now answer the questions. Use your own information.

....

....

....

....

....

4 *Pronunciation: Third person -s*

Put these words into three lists: words with /z/, /s/, and /ɪz/.

With /z/	With /s/	With /ɪz/

asks   meets
goes   practises
lives   relaxes
manages   thinks
marries   writes

5 Write the answers to these questions.

a Are Motorhead a heavy metal group? .Yes,.they.are. ....

b Does Barbra Streisand make films? ....

c Does Sade sing country music? ....

d Has Gerard Depardieu got a beard? ....

e Is Athens in Spain? ....

f Is Bill Clinton married? ....

g Does a waiter work in a bank? ....

h Do you like English? ....

6 Find responses in B to match sentences in A.

A   *B*

a I really must be going.   .... I will. Thanks.

b How's the family?   .... Yes, you must come round.

c Any news of Paula?   .... Fine. And you?

d How are you doing?   .... OK. See you.

e Let's keep in touch.   .... No, I haven't seen her for ages.

f Give my regards to George.   .... Fine, thanks.

7 Circle the word that does not belong.

a brother   uncle   nephew   (grandmother)

b aunt   children   parents   relatives

c married   father   retired   single

d sister   niece   cousin   aunt

8 Answer these questions. Use '*No, ...*' and the information in the pictures.

a Does Lisa teach Spanish?

No, she doesn't teach Spanish.

She teaches French.

b Does Jack drive a train?

....

....

c Do they work in a factory?

....

....

d Does Maria work in a shop?

....

....

e Does Julio sell shoes?

....

....

f Does Ahmed live in Cairo?

....

....

9   Use the words in brackets and make questions to ask:
    – if John and Susan have children. (Do)

    ....Do John and Susan have any children?....................................

    – what Alan's job is. (What / do)

    ....

    – the number of people in Martine's family. (How many)

    ....

    – if your friends go to university. (Do)

    ....

    – where I live. (Where)

    ....

    – if Margaret has got a sister. (Has)

    ....

10 Put the sentences in order to make a conversation.

    .... Hi, Eileen.
    .... What about you?
    .... Yes. He's got four children.
    .... Well, she doesn't have a job, but with four children she certainly works!
    .... No, I'm single. Any news of Norman?
    .... Does his wife work?
    ...1..... Hi!
    .... I haven't seen you for ages. How are things?
    .... Are you? That's great.
    .... Fine. I'm married now.

11 Rewrite the sentences. Use the words in brackets.

Example
Jack is Jane's uncle. (niece)
Jane is Jack's niece.

a I'm single. (married) ....

b Have you got any children? (Do) ....

c Michael does not have a job. (out of work) ....

d Does she have a job? (work) ....

e We don't have any children. (have / got) ....

f Liz is married to Peter. (husband) ....

g Does your niece study at the university? (student) ....

12 Translate these sentences into your language. Use a dictionary or work with someone who speaks your language.

a I have two daughters-in-law.

....

b I really must be off.

....

c Do your children go to school?

....

d Let's keep in touch.

....

e I haven't seen you for ages.

....

f Nice talking to you.

....

g Give my regards to your parents.

....

Do you ever exercise?

1 **Arrange these words in the correct order to make sentences.**

a do   on   you   what   usually   Saturday   do   ?

....

b usually   up   don't   we   early   get

....

c often   morning   go   we   the   to   town   in

....

d my   gym   to   goes   the   sometimes   wife

....

e class   always   to   Spanish   go   I   my

....

f meet   for   always   we   lunch

....

g we   shopping   often   the   do   the   afternoon   in

....

h go   night   on   never   we   out   Saturday

....

2 **Choose appropriate words to complete the sentences.**

always   usually   often   sometimes   rarely   never

a A: Do you ever go to the gym?

   B: I .... do. I go about once a month.

b A: He never walks to work.

   B: That's right. He .... drives.

c A: What time do the Spanish .... have dinner?

   B: They .... eat after 8 o'clock.

d A: Does Jill play bridge?

   B: No, she .... does. She hates it!

e A: Do you have breakfast?

   B: Yes, I .... eat breakfast but I

      .... eat lunch. I'm usually too busy!

3   Write about Jean's week. Use the correct form of the verb.

MONDAY	watch the football on TV	FRIDAY	go out with friends
TUESDAY	play tennis after work	SATURDAY	do housework and go shopping
WEDNESDAY	stay in and study	SUNDAY	play bridge with friends
THURSDAY	go to the gym at 5 o'clock		

On Monday, Jean watches the football on TV.

....

....

....

....

....

4   Write about yourself. Use these phrases.

I ... every day.
... about once a week.
... about twice a month.
... three times a ...
... four times a ...
I don't ... very much.
I don't ... very often.
I never ...

a   (write letters) ....

b   (eat out) ....

c   (exercise) ....

d   (go to the cinema) ....

e   (watch TV) ....

f   (do housework) ....

g   (meet my friends) ....

h   (cook) ....

i   (go shopping) ....

5 Which verbs go with which nouns? Write the nouns under the correct verbs.

do	go	play	watch
....	....	....	....
....	....	....	....
....	....	....	....
....	....	....	....
....	....	....	....
....	....	....	....
....	....	....	....

running   squash
aerobics   videos
sports   a football match
dancing   yoga
hiking   shopping
tennis   a play
skiing   TV
a programme   football
golf   bridge
a film   jogging
swimming   housework

6 Read the adverts. Where can you do the following?

	Hiking Club	YWCA/YMCA	Adult Education Centre
a exercise	....	....	....
b take evening classes	....	....	....
c go dancing	....	....	....
d learn a foreign language	....	....	....
e meet new people	....	....	....

■ Do you need exercise?
■ Do you enjoy walking and meeting people?

Join the Hiking Club!

■ We go on a different hike every week. Sometimes we go on a two-day hike.
■ Call **745-1191**.

Come to the YMCA or YWCA!
Look at our new activities!

aerobics squash yoga bridge club

For anyone from 9 to 90!
Singles and families.
Friday night: dance to all your favourite music.
Saturday night: oldies night!
Phone us on 235-7439.

ADULT EDUCATION CENTRE
at Woodlands School.
Mon – Fri 6.00–9.00pm.

CLASSES:
photography, computers for business, typing, Chinese cooking, Spanish, French, and Italian languages

For more information call **535-6845.**

7 **Tick the correct responses to complete the conversation.**

A: Do you get much exercise?   B: .... How often?
                               .....✓........ Yes, I do.
                               .... How about you?

A: How often do you exercise?   B: .... I watch TV a lot.
                               .... Yes, I often do.
                               .... About three times a week.

A: What do you usually do on Sunday?   B: .... I usually go swimming and play squash.
                               .... No, I never do.
                               .... I go straight home after work.

A: Where do you go swimming?   B: .... Every day from 5 to 6.
                               .... I always go to the YWCA.
                               .... No, I play tennis.

A: You're in really good shape!   .... Yes, I'm rather lazy.
                               .... Oh, are you?
                               .... Thanks a lot.

8 **Write questions using the cues below.**

When		stay in	your friends?
What		work out	at the weekend?
Where	do you	meet	lunch?
Who		see	on Saturday?
How often		eat	in the evening?
		go	for breakfast?
		do	at work?
		have	

Example
When do you usually see your friends?

....

....

....

....

....

Now answer the questions about yourself.

Example
I usually see my friends at the weekend.

....

....

....

....

....

9 Crossword puzzle: Routines

Across clues

3 Do you ... to work or take the bus?
4 I like to ... for a jog on Saturday morning.
5 We usually ... in on Mondays and watch TV.
7 On Sunday, my parents always ... ... for dinner.
10 What time do you ... work in the morning?
11 I sometimes ... fruit juice for breakfast.

Down clues

1 I rarely ... tennis; only two or three times a year.
2 They usually ... the housework on Sunday morning.
3 We often ... videos on Friday evening.
4 I usually go to bed at 11 pm and I .... at 7 am.
5 On Saturday, he usually goes to bed late and on Sunday, he often ... till midday.
6 You look so fit! How often do you ... ... ?
8 After work on Wednesday, I ... my friends and we go to the cinema.
9 I rarely walk. I prefer to ... .

10 Look at the pictures and write about Sam's day.

....

....

....

....

....

....

....

11 **Rewrite the sentences. Use the words in brackets.**

Example
I don't watch TV very much. (rarely)
I rarely watch TV.

a Every Friday, I go to the supermarket. (once / week)

....

b He keeps fit in the gym. (work out)

....

c She plays tennis a lot. (often)

....

d We never go out on Thursday evening. (stay in)

....

e I go jogging two or three times a year. (rarely)

....

f She never goes to bed early on Friday. (always / late)

....

12 **Translate these sentences into your language. Use a dictionary or work with someone who speaks your language.**

a What do you usually do on Saturday evening?

....

b Do you ever stay in bed in the morning?

....

c What do you usually do on your day off?

....

d How often do you exercise?

....

e I go for a run twice a month.

....

Did you have a good holiday?

1 Spelling check

> *Past Tense – Regular Verbs*
> Add **-ed** (most verbs): e.g. want – want**ed**
> Add **-d** (verbs ending in e): e.g. live – live**d**
> Add **-ied** (verbs ending in consonant + y): e.g. study – stud**ied**

Spell the past tense of these verbs.

a finish ....

b die ....

c dance ....

d play ....

e like ....

f listen ....

g marry ....

h phone ....

i stay ....

j try ....

k visit ....

l work ....

2 Complete the postcard. Use the past tense of the verbs below.

be   hire   do   arrive   be   stay   have   not go   be

Dear Stephanos,

Here I am in Egypt! I ....

here three days ago. I ....

a car on Tuesday and ....

some touring. I .... a

great time. Yesterday, the weather

.... awful so I

....

out. I .... very lazy and

.... in bed!

Thank you for everything in Cyprus. It

.... wonderful.

Love Gerry

3 Complete the sentences with past tense forms of *be* and *do*. Then number the sentences from 1 to 12 to make a conversation.

A

.... Oh, good! And what .... you do in Spain?

.....1..... How .... your trip?

.... you see any Spanish dancing?

.... Oh, really? I enjoy it. And .... you go to Portugal?

.... So how long .... you in Spain?

.... Where did you go?

B

.... We went to Spain. It .... great.

.... No, we .... I don't like watching. I like to dance!

.... We .... there for two weeks.

.... No, we .... We .... have time.

.... The trip .... pretty good, but the weather .... very hot.

.... Oh, we toured around, walked a lot, went swimming and

.... some shopping.

4 Write questions for these responses.

A: How ....?

B: Oh, my weekend was fine, thanks.

A: What ....?

B: Well on Saturday I went to my brother's house in Manchester. He had a party. It was fantastic!

A: That sounds good. And what ....?

B: I didn't do much on Sunday till the evening. Then I went to see the new Spielberg film.

A: Did..?

B: Yes, I enjoyed it. It's very good. Well, how about you? How ....?

A: Oh, it was terrible.

B: Really? What ....?

A: Nothing much. That was the trouble!

5 A Californian holiday

Number the sentences from a letter from 1 to 7.

.... We saw Chinatown, Fisherman's Wharf and went round San Francisco Bay in a boat.

.... Then we hired a car and drove to Palm Springs. It's about three hours from Los Angeles. We played golf there and toured around.

.... Well, that's all for now. I'll tell you everything when I get back.

.....1...... We had a great holiday in California!

.... After San Francisco, we went to Los Angeles. We loved Hollywood and Universal Studios, but I didn't like the city very much.

.... From Palm Springs, we went to San Diego. It's a beautiful city and very interesting.

.... We started our trip in San Francisco.

6 Use the cues to answer the questions with the past tense and the correct pronouns.

a Where did you buy that bag?   (in Mexico)

   I bought it in Mexico. ....

b Where did you meet your husband?   (in Portugal)

   ....

c When did you see the film?   (on Thursday night)

   ....

d Where did you get those trousers?   (in the sale at Mason's)

   ....

e When did you do your homework?   (this afternoon)

   ....

f Where did you learn French?   (in Paris)

   ....

g Where did you wait for your nephew?   (at the airport)

   ....

h When did you visit Bill and Mary?   (last week)

   ....

i What did you buy me on holiday?   (something interesting!)

   ....

7   Read the adverts for holidays below.

Skiing in Germany
Stay in 2-person flat
     10 days
          Only £350
Tel **Ski tours** 071 452 3111

Working holiday
GREECE
Are you young, fit, looking for a job?
Work in Greece – clean hotels, work in restaurants
meet tourists, etc.
3 months stay.
Call 0427 9381

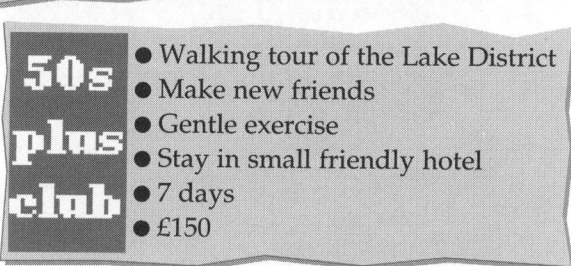

50s plus club

● Walking tour of the Lake District
● Make new friends
● Gentle exercise
● Stay in small friendly hotel
● 7 days
● £150

USA £428 rtn
★ *Disneyland*   ★ *Car hire*
★ *3 bedroom family house*
★ *Golf, tennis, swimming*   ★ *Video*
★ *Great weather*   ★ *Great touring*
Write **Family USA**, 73 Crane Street

Which holidays do you think the following people went on?

Joan, retired, single ....   Jill and Chris Chappel ....

Jim, 19, student ....   The Davidson family ....

Now write about what the people did.

Example
Jim went to Greece on a working holiday last year. He cleaned hotels, worked in restaurants and met tourists. He stayed for three months.

....

....

....

8   **Match the questions with the correct responses.**

1 Where did you go on holiday? ....   a No, we weren't with a group.

2 How long were you there? ....   b Yes, it was fine.

3 Was it a package holiday? ....   c Three days ago.

4 Did you enjoy it? ....   d We went to Italy.

5 Was the weather good? ....   e We visited museums and art galleries.

6 What did you do? ....   f Two weeks.

7 When did you get back? ....   g It was wonderful. We had a great time!

9   **Look at the page from Diane's diary. What did she do last week?**
    Write sentences.

    Example
    On Monday, she did her German homework.

    ....

    ....

    ....

    ....

    ....

    ....

    ....

    ....

    ....

    ....

    ....

    ....

    ....

MONDAY
German homework

TUESDAY
German class

WEDNESDAY
Working at home

THURSDAY
Squash after work
9pm - Good film on TV!

FRIDAY
Visit Mum
Cinema - Jo

SATURDAY
Drive to Leeds - Ann's party

SUNDAY
Write to Bank Manager
Housework

10 **Rewrite the sentences. Use the words in brackets.**

    Example
    I didn't go out on Saturday. (stay in)
    I stayed in on Saturday.

    a He didn't get up on Sunday morning. (stay in bed) ....

    b Did you have a good weekend? (How) ....

    c We travelled round the island. (tour) ....

    d I didn't do anything interesting at the weekend. (not do much) ....

    ....

    e How long were you there? (stay) ....

11 **Translate these sentences into your language. Use a dictionary or work with someone who**
    speaks your language.

    a Did you have a good holiday? ....

    b I got back here four days ago. ....

    c I stayed in all day. ....

    d How long were you there? ....

    e How was your weekend? ....

    f It was wonderful! ....

You can't miss it!

1 **Use the map to answer the questions. Use these prepositions.**

behind   near   next to   in   on the corner of   opposite   between

a Where's the nearest bank?

   There's one on the corner. ....

b Is there a post office near here?

   ....

c I'm looking for a chemist's.

   ....

d Where's the Star Hotel?

   ....

e Is there a library around here?

   ....

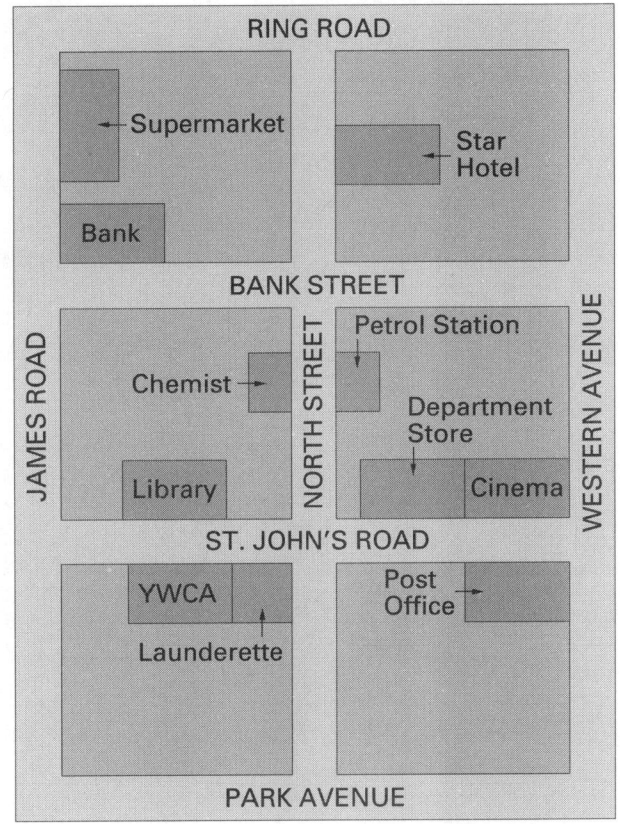

2 **Find responses in B to match the questions in A.**

A

a What's your new house like?

b How big is it?

c What's the neighbourhood like?

d Is there a bus stop nearby?

B

.... Yes, I like it.

....✓.... It's really nice.

.... Yes, it is.

.... It has five rooms.

.... Yes, it's very big.

.... No, it's not very big.

.... They are very interesting.

.... Yes, I like them.

.... It's very quiet.

.... Yes, there are.

.... Yes, on the corner of the street.

.... Yes, it is.

3 **Look at these two street maps. There are ten differences between them. Two differences are given below as examples. Find the other eight.**

There are some trees in North Street in A, but there aren't any in B.
There is a park on the corner of Parks Road and West Road in A, but there isn't one in B.
In B, there is a car park.

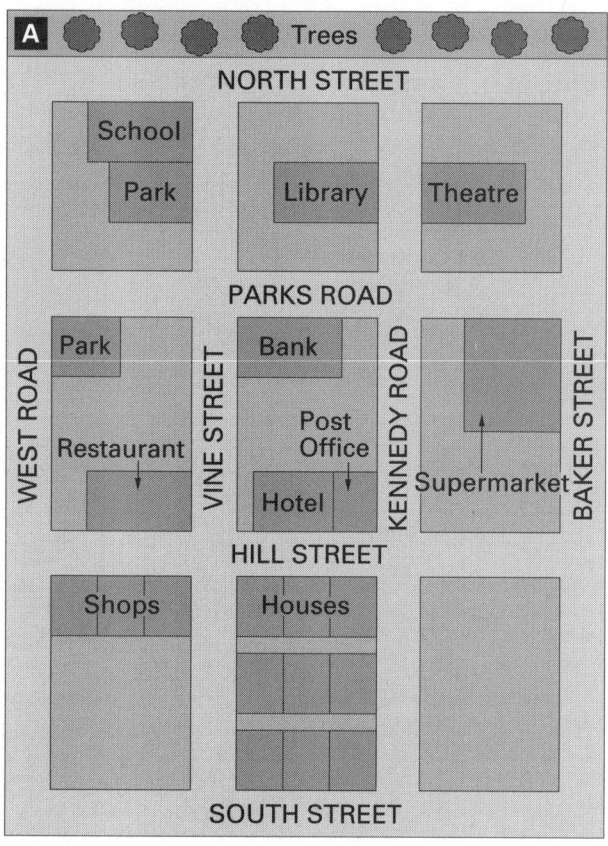
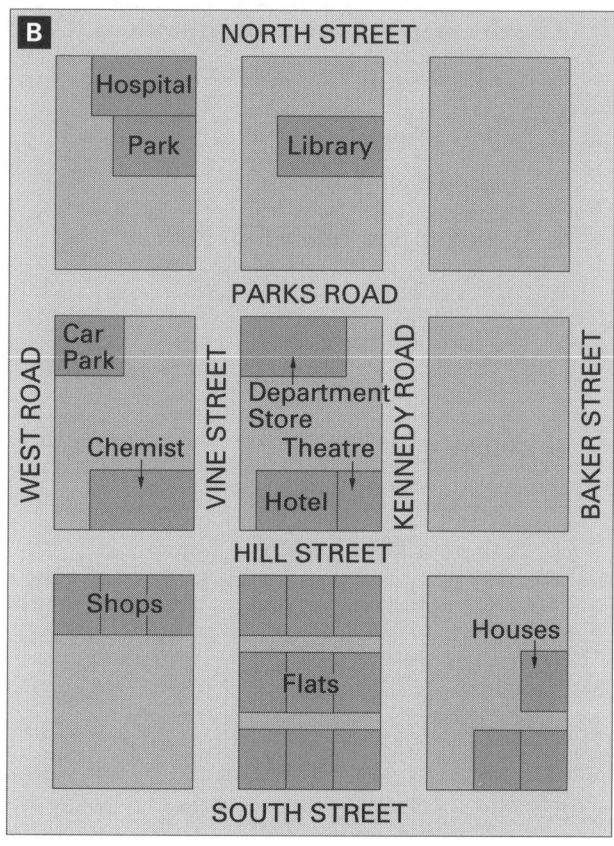

....

....

....

....

....

....

....

....

....

....

....

....

....

....

4   Underline one wrong thing in each advertisement.

To let: Large house in quiet location. Near schools and convenient for public transport. Suit family with children. Next to motorway and airport.
Telephone Mary Winslow 943 5984

Small studio flat available

5 bedrooms

Phone 862 342

LARGE, 4 BEDROOM HOUSE IN QUIET NEIGHBOURHOOD. AVAILABLE FROM FEBRUARY 15TH.
NEAR SCHOOL AND SHOPS.
SUIT SINGLE, PROFESSIONAL PERSON.
BOX 54

Room to rent in town house. Fully furnished. T.V. Shared bathroom and kitchen. Suit family with children.
Phone Mrs Smith (mornings).
Tel 398 4357

New house in Elm Avenue. Only £800 a month. 4 bedrooms, garage and garden. House 150 years old but in good condition.
Contact Jenkins Brothers.

Flat to rent. Very cheap. Two bedrooms, bathroom and kitchen.

Only £600 a week.

Call: 952 327

5   Crossword puzzle: Places

Across clues

2 I like to see plays at the ... .
3 Is there a bus ... nearby?
8 We always wash our clothes on Saturday at the ... .
10 I want some medicine. I need to go to the ... .
11 A ... is a place where you borrow books.
12 I need to telephone my parents. Is there a ... box near here?

Down clues

1 I love Mexican food. Is there a good Mexican ... in the neighbourhood?
2 He works for a ... agent's and takes people on tours.
4 A ... ... is a place where you get stamps and post letters.
5 The Ritzy is a very good ... for foreign films.
6 I need some money. Is there a ... near here?
7 Do you like art? There's a good art ... nearby.
9 What ... do your children go to?

6 **Where can you do the following things? Match the descriptions with the places. Then write sentences.**

a buy some groceries   ......d...... post office
b get some books   .... supermarket
c get some petrol   .... bus stop
d buy some stamps   .... gym
e catch a bus   .... launderette
f wash some clothes   .... bookshop
g telephone a friend   .... phone box
h keep fit   .... petrol station
i buy a newspaper   .... newsagent's

...A post office is a place where you can buy stamps.....................

....

....

....

....

....

....

7 **Answer the questions about your neighbourhood like this:**

Yes, there is. There's one in/near/opposite ...
No, there isn't.
Yes, there are. There are some next to/behind/between ...
No, there aren't.

a Are there any good restaurants around here?

....

b Is there a good theatre nearby?

....

c Is there a phone near here?

....

d Are there any good clothes shops?

....

e Is there a post office?

....

f Is there a police station near the school?

....

g Are there any good bookshops?

....

8   **Rewrite the sentences. Use the words in brackets.**

Example
Is there a petrol station near here? (nearby)
Is there a petrol station nearby?

a   I'm new around here. (just moved in)

....

b   The library is next to the post office and the bank. (between)

....

c   Yes, there's a garage on the corner. (one)

....

d   My house is near the station. (convenient)

....

e   It has a garden too. (also)

....

f   I like it a lot. (really)

....

g   Yes, there are shops in Pine Road. (some)

....

9   **Translate these sentences into your language. Use a dictionary or work with someone who speaks your language.**

a   I'm not sure.

....

b   The chemist's is on the corner.

....

c   I've just moved in.

....

d   By the way, is there a good restaurant round here?

....

e   What is your new flat like?

....

f   My house is convenient for public transport.

....

g   Sorry, I don't know.

....

What's she wearing?

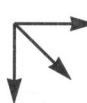

1 Find 14 clothes and accessories.

j	u	m	p	e	r	a	t	b	e	l	t
a	e	x	i	e	m	l	q	t	w	d	v
c	s	a	h	r	m	g	p	k	i	r	d
k	h	s	n	e	c	k	l	a	c	e	w
e	i	h	l	s	c	q	w	o	u	s	p
t	r	o	u	s	e	r	s	b	v	s	t
l	t	e	f	n	z	r	i	u	h	e	a
f	j	s	k	i	r	t	d	n	y	p	s
b	r	a	c	e	l	e	t	v	g	e	l

How many words can you list in each category?

Women only   *Men and women*   *Men only*

2 *Spelling check: Verb + -ing*

> Add **-ing** (most verbs):   walk – walk**ing**
> Drop e and add **-ing:**   give – giv**ing**
> Double the final consonant and add **-ing:**   sit – sit**ting**

Write the *-ing* form of these verbs.

come ....   have ....   run ....

swim ....   do ....   help ....

sell ....   take ....   get ....

love ....   drive ....   work ....

3 **Find the opposites.**

a big	e good	.... bad	.... noisy
b old	f quiet	.... boring	.... small
c cheap	g straight	.... curly	.... tall
d short	h exciting	.... expensive	.... young

4 Complete these descriptions. Use the present continuous and the verbs below. Remember to use the correct form of the verb **be**.

a   sell   sit   wash   wait   talk   stand   read   jog   dry

Some people .... at a bus stop. A woman ....

.... to a taxi driver. A man .... some newspapers.

A young man .... next to him. He ....

.... a newspaper. Two women .... Some people

.... in a launderette. They ....

and .... their clothes.

b   talk   eat   listen   dance   sit   stand   drink

Jim and Sandy .... Mario ....

.... between Angela and Helmut. He ....

.... to Angela. Helmut .... Carlos

.... behind them. He ....

and .... to their conversation.

5 Circle the things in each description that do not match the picture. Then write the correct information.

a She's about 12. She's got straight fair hair. She's wearing jeans and is carrying a book.

....

b He's in his thirties. He is quite tall and has dark, curly hair. He is wearing jeans and a T-shirt.

....

c She's got long hair and is wearing a T-shirt and skirt. She's playing tennis.

....

6 Complete the conversations with questions in the present continuous.

A: Which one is Mark? What ....?

B: A red shirt and jeans.

A: Where .... (go)?

B: I .... to the shops. Do you want anything?

A: Who .... (talk to)?

B: She .... (talk to) her cousin.

A: Is Kate in her office?

B: No, ... lunch.

A: What .... you .... (write)?

B: A postcard to my grandmother.

A: .... you and Sam .... (watch) TV?

B: No, ... a video.

7   *About me*

Answer these questions.

1 Are you sitting down? ....

2 What are you doing? ....

3 Are you working hard? ....

4 Where are you studying? ....

5 What are you wearing?

....

....

6 What do you look like?

....

....

8   Describe the people below.

....

....

....

....

....

....

....

....

9 **Rewrite the sentences. Use the words in brackets.**

Example
His hair is straight and black. (got)
He's got straight, black hair.

a She is 25 years old. (twenties)

....

b She's studying engineering at university. (read)

....

c He's not tall and not short. (medium)

....

d Has she got blonde hair? (Does)

....

e He's quite tall. (fairly)

....

10 **Translate these sentences into your language. Use a dictionary or work with someone who speaks your language.**

1 Tom is working late tonight.

....

2 Which one is Sarah?

....

3 He's reading economics at university.

....

4 She's in her thirties.

....

5 What does she look like?

....

6 He's fairly tall with dark hair and a beard.

....

Have you ever ... ?

1 Complete the verb table. Use a dictionary to help you if necessary.

Present	Past	Past participle
be	was	been
give	....	given
drive	drove	....
forget	....	....
go	....	gone
....	knew	....
see	....	....
....	....	taken

2 Have you ever done any of these things? Tick (✔) the ones that you have done.

.... a seen a UFO
.... b had an accident
.... c eaten Malaysian food
.... d driven a sports car
.... e been to a concert
.... f worked in a foreign country
.... g seen a famous person
.... h helped a stranger
.... i travelled round the world
.... j lost your luggage

Now write sentences about the things you have and haven't done (with *not* and *never*).
Give details.

a   I have seen a UFO, I think. It was near my home. It was big and yellow. ....

b   ....

c   ....

d   ....

e   ....

f   ....

g   ....

h   ....

i   ....

j   ....

3 Jan likes to visit other countries and go sightseeing. Use the map and pictures below to write about him.

Example
Jan has been to France but he hasn't been to England.

....

....

....

....

....

....

....

....

4 Match the questions with the correct responses.

a Have you been to Italy?

b When was the last time you went?

c Did you visit Venice?

d No, I've never been to Venice but I've read a lot about it. Have you read *Death in Venice?*

.... Two months ago.

.... No, I haven't. But I've seen the film.

.... Yes, I have. I've been there four times.

.... Yes, I did. What about you? Have you been there?

5 A terrible time!

What happened? Read this description and number the events from 1 to 9 in the order they occurred.

.... I ate lunch and then found I didn't have enough money!

.... She was very nice and brought some money to the restaurant.

.... After that, I called my sister but she was out too.

......1...... I had a terrible time on Saturday.

.... First, I called my parents but they were out.

.... So finally I called my neighbour at home.

.... I went out to do some shopping then I went to a restaurant for lunch.

.... Then I tried my friend but he was out too.

.... It was awful. Next time, I'll eat at home!

6 Write questions to match the responses. Use *Have you ever ... ?* or *Have you ... ?*

....

a Yes, I was in a car accident last week.

....

b No, I've never been there.

....

c Yes, I forgot my brother's wedding and I was late.

....

d No, I've never tried it.

....

e Yes, I've driven one. It was fantastic!

....

f No, I've never lost it.

7 Write the nouns under the correct verbs.

drive	*have*	*ride*	*take*
....	....	....	....
....	....	....	....
....	....	....	....
....	....	....	....
....	....	....	....

a holiday   an accident
a car   a flight
a taxi   a trip
a van   a bicycle
a train   a bus
a lorry   a motorcycle

8 Crossword puzzle: Present perfect

Complete the crossword with the correct form of the appropriate verb.

Across clues

Have you ever ...

2 ... something you didn't want at a car boot sale?
4 ... to do your homework?
6 ... someone famous?
7 ... English to an American?
8 ... a sports car?
12 ... aerobics for 3 hours?
13 ... a UFO?

Down clues

Have you ever ...

1 ... anything for a good price in a sale?
3 ... your passport in a foreign country?
5 ... a taxi to an airport?
9 ... a motorbike?
10 ... Vietnamese food?
11 ... on a package holiday?

9 A strange thing happened to Jill last week! Write the story that the pictures tell. Use the words below where appropriate.

after that   next   then   finally

....

....

....

....

....

....

10 Rewrite the sentences. Use the words in brackets in the correct form.

1 Have you ever been round the world? (travel)

....

2 I haven't eaten Thai food. (never / try)

....

3 I have owned two motorbikes and a car. (have)

....

4 Have you ever had a car accident? (be / in)

....

5 She has never had a speeding ticket. (get)

....

11 Translate these sentences into your language. Use a dictionary or work with someone who speaks your language.

1 A strange thing happened to me last week.

....

2 Then what did you do?

....

3 Have you ever seen anything unusual?

....

4 That's not what worries me!

....

5 Slow down a bit.

....

You should go in spring

1 **Put the words in B's answers in the correct order.**

A: Is your home town a nice place?
B: beautiful   and   yes   it's   beach
   an   has   excellent   it

....

....

A: What's the weather like?
B: the   very   it's   summer   hot   in

....

....

A: And how about in the winter?
B: it's   winter   cold   in   very

....

A: Is it an interesting town?
B: and   a   to   university   and   there's   lots   do   theatre   yes   a

....

A: Is it expensive there?
B: not   and   no   too   cheap   rents   expensive   it's   are

....

2 **Choose the correct word to complete each statement.**

a You spend a lot of money in New York City.

Everything is pretty .... there.

(cheap, expensive, big)

b My home town is not an exciting place. It is really

.... (fascinating, interesting, boring)

c Rome is a beautiful, old city. There are not many

.... buildings. (big, modern, small)

d This city is fairly dangerous. It is not very

.... at night. (safe, noisy, quiet)

e Athens is a quiet city in the winter. The streets

are never .... at that time of year.

(clean, safe, crowded)

3 **Read about these cities. Underline the information in each description that doesn't agree.**

Los Angeles is a famous city in California. It is famous for its film stars, roads and restaurants. It has excellent museums, universities and shopping centres. The weather is often quite cold.
Tourists like to go to the film studios and to drive along Hollywood Boulevard. Los Angeles has a warm climate and good beaches nearby.

Tokyo is Japan's exciting capital city. It is a place where old Japan meets modern Japan, with beautiful buildings and fascinating old temples. It is a very busy city. It is also one of the most expensive cities in the world. A room in a good hotel only costs a few pounds.

4 *On holiday*

Give advice with *should* and *shouldn't* using the sentences below.

a Take a bus tour of the city.

   You should take a bus tour of the city.

b Don't stay near the airport.

   ....

c Go in the spring or summer.

   ....

d Don't walk alone late at night.

   ....

e See the Eiffel Tower.

   ....

f It rains a lot so take an umbrella.

   ....

g It's quite cold so take a jumper.

   ....

h Don't go in the winter. It's very cold then.

   ....

i Don't miss St Paul's. It's a beautiful building.

   ....

5   Use *and* or *but* to join the sentences.

> Use **and** for additional information: It is a beautiful city **and** it has a good climate.
> Use **but** for contrasting information: It is a very old city **but** it has a
>   modern shopping centre.

a   Paris is a very interesting place. It has some beautiful buildings.

Paris is a very interesting place and it has some beautiful buildings.

b   London is an exciting city. It has great night clubs.

....

....

c   My home town is a beautiful place. The climate is
    too cold for me in the winter.

....

....

d   Australia is a beautiful country. It has a very
    good climate.

....

....

e   Rome is an exciting place for a holiday. It is very good for shopping.

....

f   York does not have a very good climate. It is a very interesting place to visit.

....

6   Circle the word that does not belong.

a   old   (small)   modern   new
b   fascinating   interesting   wonderful   boring   exciting
c   nice   noisy   dirty   dangerous   ugly
d   hot   wet   ugly   cold   dry
e   fantastic   excellent   wonderful   great   awful

7   Tick (✔) if the sentences need *a* or *an*. Then add *a* or *an* where necessary.

> Use **a** or **an** with adjective + singular noun: It is **an old city**.
>   It has **a new park**.
> Use no article with **be** + adjective: It is old.

a   .... Restaurants are very cheap in Mexico.

b   ..✔.. Copenhagen is ₐᵃ clean city.

c   .... Sydney Harbour is beautiful.

d   .... Dallas has big airport.

e   .... Flats are expensive in Milan.

f   .... Barcelona is crowded city in summer.

g   .... London has good museums.

h   .... Spain is exciting country to visit.

8 **Complete this description of London with *is* or *has*.**

London .... Britain's biggest city. It .... a very old capital.

It .... a city of interesting architecture and it .... many beautiful parks.

It also .... some excellent theatres and museums.

London .... very crowded in summer.

It .... a popular city with foreign tourists and .... more than eight million visitors a year.

The city .... famous for its shopping and .... many excellent department stores.

London .... convenient trains and buses which cross the city so it .... easy for tourists to get around. There are a lot of good restaurants in London. There .... British food, of course, and London .... lots of excellent Indian, Chinese, Japanese, French, Italian and Greek restaurants.

9 **Match the descriptions of the places with the photos.**

a

> My home town, Brighton, is great. When the weather is fine we can go to the beach and when it isn't there is still lots to do in town and on the seafront. There are shops, cafes, clubs, restaurants, parks, really interesting buildings and every year there's an arts festival.

1 ....

b

> I'm from Liverpool, an exciting city, I think. I like the museums, art galleries, shops and night clubs but most of all, I like the people. They're fantastic! This is good because it's a very crowded city!

2 ....

c

> I live in a beautiful Essex village called Thaxted. It has an interesting and very big church, old streets and buildings and a small museum. There are lots of events. There's a music festival in the summer and morris dancing in early June. I'm a member of the morris dancing team.

3 ....

10 Now write a description of your home town.

....

....

....

....

....

....

11 Rewrite the sentences. Use the words in brackets.

Example
Tell me about your home town. (What / like)
What's your home town like?

a It is always sunny and warm. (The climate)

....

b There are always a lot of people in the streets.
(The streets / crowded)

....

c It's a rather expensive city. (not cheap)

....

d Take a lot of money with you. (should)

....

e It's not a very interesting place. (rather / boring)

....

12 Translate these sentences into your language.
Use a dictionary or work with someone who speaks
your language.

a What's your home town like?

....

b The climate is pretty good.

....

c It's not a very crowded city.

....

d I suppose it is rather expensive.

....

e You should go in spring.

....

Stay in bed!

1   Match the words and definitions.

a chemist's   e indigestion
b shampoo   f ointment
c toothpaste   g soap
d medicine   h insomnia

.... a pain in your stomach after
          you've eaten
.... something you clean your
          teeth with
.... when you cannot sleep
.... something you wash your
          hair with
.... a place where you buy medicine
.... something you take when you're ill
.... something you wash your body with
.... cream

2   Rewrite the requests below. Use *can, could* or *would*.

Can I have ..., please?   I'd like ..., please.
Could I have ..., please?   I would like ..., please.

a Give me something for a headache.

....

b Give me some vitamin tablets.

....

c I need some throat pastilles.

....

d I want a box of tissues.

....

e Give me a large tube of toothpaste.

....

f I want a small jar of cream.

....

g Give me a bottle of aspirins.

....

h I need something for the flu.

....

3 **Draw a line from each phrase to words in the list. How many connections can you make for each phrase?**

shampoo

hairspray

deodorant

a bottle of   aftershave   a jar of

a box of   shaving cream   a bar of

a can of   sunburn lotion   a pack of

a stick of   tablets   a tube of

tissues

toothpaste

aspirins

soap

4 **Use *should* and the phrases below to give advice for each problem.**

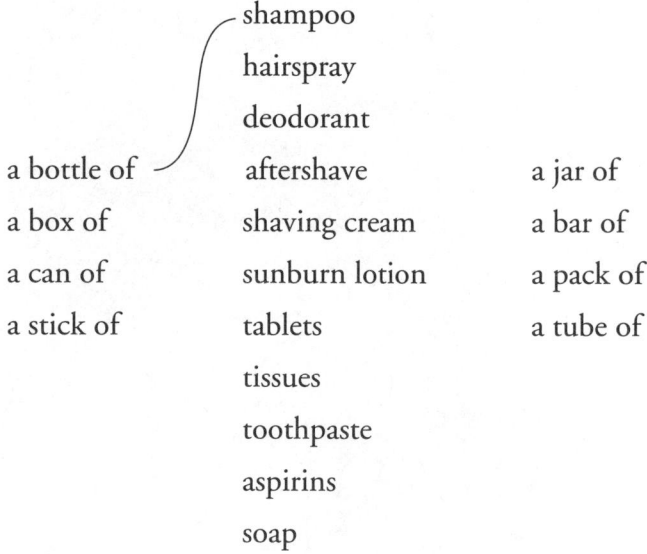

... drink hot chicken soup

... take an aspirin

... put lotion on it

... take some cough medicine

... stay in bed and rest

... drink water with baking soda

... drink warm milk

a a backache ...For a backache, you should stay in bed and rest. ....

b a headache ....

c a cold ....

d indigestion ....

e a cough ....

f insomnia ....

g sunburn ....

5   Read this passage. Then circle T (true) or F (false) for the statements below.

Getting to sleep

Usually, people sleep between seven and eight hours a day, although some people need less than this and some need more. But millions of people have trouble getting to sleep every night.

Many people do not know why they have insomnia. Most people know that tea and coffee often make it difficult to go to sleep because they contain caffeine. But some medicines, such as cold tablets, also contain caffeine. Sleeping pills can help you fall asleep, but when you wake up the next morning you feel tired.

You will sleep more easily if your bedroom is used only for sleep. You shouldn't use your bedroom as an office, a TV room or an exercise room. You should also have a regular sleeping routine but don't go to bed until you are tired. Try to go to bed at the same time every night and get up at the same time every morning. Don't eat just before you go to bed but try a glass of warm milk. And if all this doesn't work, try counting sheep!

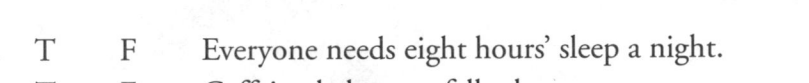

a   T   F   Everyone needs eight hours' sleep a night.
b   T   F   Caffeine helps you fall asleep.
c   T   F   You shouldn't work in your bedroom.
d   T   F   You shouldn't drink anything before you go to bed.
e   T   F   It is good to have a TV near your bed.
f   T   F   You should have regular sleeping hours.

6   Choose the correct preposition to complete the conversation.

A: I need something .... insomnia. (for / on / with)

B: Try these tablets. Take two .... the evening. (at / in / on) And don't drink a lot .... coffee. (at / for / of)

A: OK. Thank you.

B: And sometimes warm milk helps you go .... sleep. (for / in / to)

A: Really? I'll try it.

B: Anything else?

A: Yes, can I have a bottle .... sleeping tablets, please? (of / to / with)

B: Oh, you should talk .... your doctor to get that. (for / to / at)

7 Crossword puzzle

Across clues

1 For good ... you need enough vitamins, exercise and sleep.
4 I've got a sore throat and a cough. I think I've caught a ... .
7 You put food in this part of the body.
8 I've got a cold or a touch of ... .
9 I lifted two very heavy bags yesterday and today
  I've got ... .
12 You listen with this part of the body.

Down clues

2 I've got something in my left ... . It hurts when I open it.
3 He's got terrible ... . He's gone to see a dentist.
5 I've got a dreadful cold. My head hurts, my body hurts,
  I've got a sore throat and a bad ... .
6 I stayed in the sun too long! I've got ... .
7 I'd like some pastilles or some .... for a sore throat, please.
10 The part of the body between the foot and the leg.
11 He's always tired and doesn't have any ... these days.

8 What is wrong with the people below? Give them advice.

a He's got a headache. He should take some
  aspirins.

b ....

c ....

d ....

e ....

f ....

9 **Rewrite the sentences. Use the words in brackets.**

Example
I've got a bad backache. (pain)
I've got a bad pain in my back.

a Stay in bed! (not / get up)

....

b Stay in. (should not / go out)

....

c You should eat nothing. (Don't)

....

d I want some aspirins, please. (would like)

....

e You shouldn't lift anything heavy. (Don't)

....

10 **Translate these sentences into your language. Use a dictionary or work with someone who speaks your language.**

a I've got a touch of flu.

....

b Don't get up for two days.

....

c Don't catch cold.

....

d Can you recommend something for a sore throat?

....

e Take it easy.

....

f I think you should see a dentist.

....

May I take your order, please?

1 Use one or more words to complete the conversation between a waiter and a customer.

A: May I .... your order, please?

B: Yes, ... a steak, please. I'd like it well done.

A: And .... you like a salad?

B: Yes, ...

A: What ....
dressing would you like?

B: French, please.

A: Would .... drink?

B: Yes, ... coffee,
....

A: Anything else?

B: No, ... all, thanks.

2 Put the menu items into the categories below. Use a dictionary to help you, if necessary.

apple pie	baked fish	bananas	bread	beef	carrots
cheesecake	coffee	french fries	fresh peas	fried chicken	green salad
ice cream	mashed potatoes	onion soup	oranges	pasta	rice
sandwich	spaghetti	steak	strawberry	turkey	tea
water	yogurt				

Side orders   *Starters/Appetizers*   *Drinks*

Desserts   *Vegetables*   *Meat/Fish*   *Fruit*

3 Choose the best response.

a Would you like anything else?   ......√....... Not right now, thanks.
.... You're welcome.
.... Not at all.

b How about the grilled salmon with new potatoes?   .... That'll be fine.
.... What will you have?
.... Not too bad, thanks.

c So that's a table for four at eight o'clock.   .... Can I see the menu?
.... Not at all.
.... That's right.

d May I take your order?   .... Of course not.
.... Not at all.
.... Yes, the steak for me, please.

e And what would you like to drink with your meal?   .... Yes, please.
.... Water, please.
.... I'll have the fish, please.

4 Gina wants a pizza delivered to her home. Complete the telephone conversation.

A: Hello. Fast Pizza. May ....?

B: I'd like to order a pizza, please.

A: Certainly. Would ....?

B: No, not a large one. I'd like a small one.

A: What kind of ....?

B: I'd like one with cheese, olive and sausage.

A: Fine. And would ....?

B: Yes, I'll have a large cola, please.

A: Could ....?

B: My name's Gina Lanzo. And my phone number is 821 3003.

A: And may ....?

B: My address is 238 Oak Street.

A: OK. We'll bring your pizza in twenty minutes.

B: Thanks. Bye.

5 Read the description of what usually happens when you eat at a restaurant. Number
the sentences from 1 to 10 in the order each event usually happens.

.... The cook prepares your meal.

.... The waitress/waiter brings you a menu.

.... The waitress/waiter brings your bill and then
you pay the bill and leave.

.... The waitress/waiter takes you to a table
and you sit down.

.... The waitress/waiter then brings your meal.

.... You read the menu and decide what you
want to eat and drink.

.... Then she/he takes the order to the kitchen.

.... When you are ready to leave, you ask for the bill.

.... You tell the waitress/waiter what you want and
she/he writes down your order.

.... You eat your meal.

6 Choose the best word to complete the sentences below.

a In a restaurant, the waitress/waiter takes your .... (menu, order, service)

b At many restaurants, you should make a(n) .... before you go.
(order, reservation, menu)

c Many people like .... on their salad. (dessert, dressing, soup)

d In most restaurants, you can have three .... ; a starter, a main meal
and a dessert. (meals, courses, dishes)

e It is very important for a restaurant to have good .... as well as good food
and drink. (service, telephones, reservations)

f At a good restaurant, the service is .... (quick, rude, slow), the food

is .... (tasty, undercooked, greasy), and the cost of a meal is

.... (reasonable, expensive, clean).

7 Use the cue words below to form the waitress's questions.

Example
like / drink / meal ?   *Would you like a drink with your meal?*

a name / address / phone number ? ....

b take / order / please ? ....

c water ? ....

d How / like / steak ? ....

e kind / potatoes / like ? ....

f anything else ? ....

Now write appropriate short answers for the questions.

a ....   b ....

c ....   d ....

e ....   f ....

8 Read the adverts and then answer the questions.

DYNASTY RESTAURANT

2nd floor, Ward Shopping Centre
Open 11 am to 10 pm
7 days a week
Excellent Chinese cuisine
Shrimp with lobster sauce
Spicy fried beef or chicken
Lemon chicken
Vegetarian orders also available.

Eat in or take out!

For **free** delivery call **922 4856**

Come to the
Yum Yum Restaurant!

Breakfast, lunch, dinner

Open 24 hours

Family restaurant

Our specialities – desserts:
freshly baked pies & cakes daily.

Set menu: £10

Visa and **Mastercard** welcome.

Sorry, no delivery.

49 High Street, Kingston

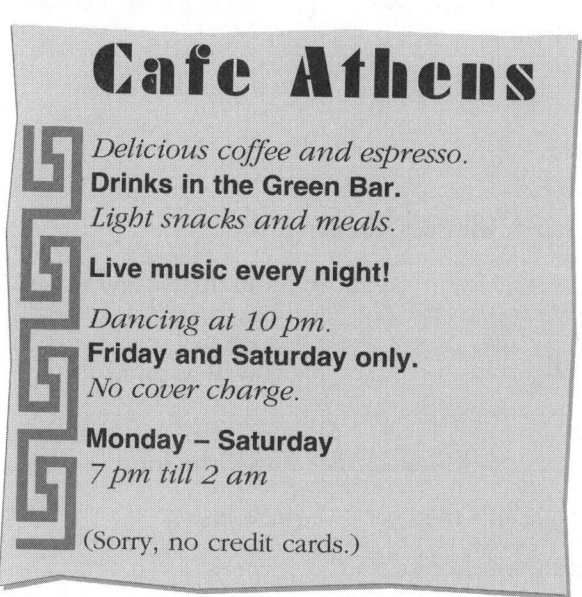

Cafe Athens

Delicious coffee and espresso.
Drinks in the Green Bar.
Light snacks and meals.

Live music every night!

Dancing at 10 pm.
Friday and Saturday only.
No cover charge.

Monday – Saturday
7 pm till 2 am

(Sorry, no credit cards.)

GIORGIO'S

Italian Restaurant, 14 Holland Street
647 99928 for reservations

Lunch & Dinner Service
Monday – Saturday
11.30 am – 11.30 pm

Spaghetti, lasagne, pizza:
the best in town!
Outdoor seating available.

Reservations necessary.

Most credit cards accepted.
All meals cooked to order by our famous chef,
Giorgio.

a Which restaurant is open at 3 am? ....

b Which restaurant has Italian food? ....

c Which restaurant serves breakfast? ....

d Which restaurant has entertainment? ....

e Which restaurants are open on Sunday? ....

f Which restaurant delivers meals to your home? ....

9 **Match the adjectives on the right with appropriate nouns on the left.**
   (There may be more than one correct response.)

a waiters .... tough
b service .... expensive
c restaurant .... undercooked
d chicken .... dirty
e vegetables .... cold

f apple pie .... busy
g coffee .... salty
h meal .... unfriendly
i tables .... slow
j soup .... tasteless

10 Now use the nouns and adjectives you matched in Exercise 9 to write a review of *The Greasy Spoon*, a terrible restaurant!

Start like this:

I had dinner with a friend at The Greasy Spoon Restaurant last week.

....

....

....

....

11 Rewrite the sentences. Use the words in brackets.

Example
What's your name? (Could)
Could I have your name, please?

1 Would you like to order? (May / take)

....

2 What would you like for dessert? (will / have)

....

3 Do you have a table for two on Saturday, please? (would like)

....

4 What kind of ice cream would you like? (flavour)

....

5 I'll have the chicken, please. ('d like)

....

12 Translate these sentences into your language. Use a dictionary or work with someone who speaks your language.

1 I'd like to reserve a table, please. ....

2 What will you have to drink? ....

3 What flavour would you like? ....

4 What do you recommend? ....

5 How would you like your steak? ....

6 That'll be all, thank you. ....

14 It's the best!

1 Match each word with a definition.

a beach
b desert
c wood
d island
e lake
f mountain
g ocean

.... a large area of land covered with trees

.... the area where the sea meets the land, usually with sand or rocks

.... an area of water with land all around it

.... a dry, sandy place where it doesn't rain much and there aren't many plants

.... an area of salt water which covers a large part of the earth

.... a piece of land with water all around it

.... a very big hill, often with snow on top

2 Spelling check: comparatives

Add -er:	cheap – cheaper
Add -r:	nice – nicer
Drop y and add -ier:	dirty – dirtier
Double the final consonant and add -er:	hot – hotter

Write the comparative forms of these adjectives.

a hot ....

b sunny ....

c healthy ....

d empty ....

e small ....

f nice ....

g cold ....

h large ....

i warm ....

Now complete the sentences.

a London is big but Tokyo is .... (big).

b Town life is .... (busy) than country life.

c I think people in small towns are .... (friendly) than in big cities.

d The North of England is .... (wet) than the South.

3   Write questions using the cues below and the comparative forms of the adjectives.

   a   Which is .... (big), London or Paris?

   b   Which is .... (modern), Brasilia or Tokyo?

   c   Where do people live .... (long), Japan or the USA?

   d   Which is .... (old), Budapest or Warsaw?

   e   Which is .... (hot) in summer, Egypt or Jordan?

   f   Which is .... (exciting), New York or Madrid?

   g   Which is .... (cheap), Portugal or Germany?

   h   Which is .... (cold), Italy or Norway?

Do you know the answers to the questions?

4   Use the words in the box to complete the statements below.

Adjective	Comparative	Superlative
good	better	best
bad	worse	worst

   a   The weather was terrible in Belgium. But we enjoyed France because the weather was
much .... there.

   b   It was a horrible trip across the Channel. In fact, it was the .... trip I've ever had.

   c   The Park Hotel is a .... place to stay. It's not expensive and it's in the
city centre.

   d   July is a .... month to travel in Europe than September. All the hotels are full
and the trains are very crowded.

   e   Turkey has some of the .... beaches in the world. They are wonderful!

5   Complete the table below.

large	....	largest
....	drier	....
big	....	....
....	longer	....
expensive	....	....

Now use words from the table to complete the statements below.

   a   The .... continent is Asia.

   b   The .... river is the Nile.

   c   The .... place is the Atacama Desert in Chile.

   d   China has the .... population in the world.

   e   Hotels in London are .... than hotels in Paris, but hotels in Tokyo are the
.... of all.

6 Crossword puzzle: Did you know?

Across clues

1 Hotels in Paris are ... than hotels in London.
3 Do you think it is ... in Granada in June or September?
4 I think people in the country are ... than in the towns.
5 The ... parts of most towns are more interesting than the modern ones.
9 The weather is terrible in winter. It's ... in the spring.
10 There isn't much to see here. It's not a very ... place.
11 Which is the ... place in the winter: Stockholm, Helsinki or Moscow?
14 I think New York is the most ... city in the world.
15 Life in the city is too noisy and too ... for me. I like peace and quiet.
16 The Vatican City is the ... country in the world. It only has 800 people.

Down clues

2 Tokyo is the most ... city in the world.
3 Your bag is very heavy but mine is even ... .
4 Venice is the most ... city I have ever visited. It's wonderful!
6 The Pacific is the ... ocean in the world.
7 K2 is not the ... mountain.
8 It's much ... by the sea. It's much too hot in the valleys.
12 Life in the East and life in the West is very ... .
13 I had a ... holiday! The weather was cold and the hotel was expensive.

7 Write sentences of fact using the cues below.

1 Mount Everest   (high)

....

2 University of Bologna and University of Oxford   (old)

....

3 San Francisco airport and London Heathrow   (not busy)

....

4 Sears Tower   (tall)

....

5 France and England   (large)

....

6 Spain and North Pole   (cold)

....

8   **Read about the countries below. Find one thing wrong in each description.**

Australia is an island continent in the South Pacific. The capital is Canberra, but the city with the biggest population is Sydney, which has nearly four million. English is the first language of most people, but there are also many people who speak English as a second language. Indonesia is one of Australia's nearest neighbours. It is only a short flight from the northern city of Darwin, Australia's biggest city.

Canada is the second largest country in land size. It stretches 3,223 miles from east to west, and from the North Pole to the US border. Canada has a warm climate all year round. Both English and French are official languages. Many French-speaking people live in the province of Quebec, where Montreal is the biggest city. Canada has a cold winter, and many Canadians enjoy winter sports, such as skiing and ice skating.

Switzerland is a small country in central Europe. Its neighbours are France in the west, Italy in the south, Austria in the east, and Germany in the north. Sixty per cent of the land is mountains. Switzerland is famous for its banks, tourism and skiing. It's a very easy place to walk or drive around because there are no hills.

9   **Look at the photos of a small British village, a small seaside town and a large city. Write five sentences comparing the places.**

Newquay

West Tanfield

Birmingham

Example
West Tanfield is smaller than Birmingham.

....

....

....

....

....

10 Rewrite the sentences. Use the words in brackets.

Example
London is safer than New York.   (not / dangerous)
London is not as dangerous as New York.

1 London is safer than New York. (dangerous)

....

2 Flats in Portugal are cheaper than flats in Germany. (expensive)

....

3 Japanese food is better for you than Western food. (healthy)

....

4 I think life in the country is quieter than life in the city. (noisy)

....

5 City life is much more exciting than country life. (boring)

....

11 Translate these sentences into your language. Use a dictionary or work with someone who speaks your language.

1 Country life is less exciting than city life.

....

2 City life is much more expensive than country life.

....

3 Country life is not as expensive as city life.

....

4 Asia is the largest continent in the world.

....

5 What's the most populated country in the world?

....

Please tell her I called

1 Complete this telephone conversation.

A: Hello. Alphisa, ... you?

B: Yes, could you .... to Raymond Snyder, please?

A: Certainly. Who's ....?

B: Josette Stewart at Mallid's.

A: ...., please. I'm sorry, the number ....

 Can I .... a message?

B: Can you .... him I ....,

 please and .... him to ....

 a ring. I'm at the George Hotel, Room 603.

A: OK. I ....

B: Thank you. Goodbye.

A: ....

2 Choose the correct responses for the questions.

a Would you like to hold?	.... Yes, please. Could you tell him Ros Baker called?
b Who's calling?	.... Never mind. I'll call back.
c Can I take a message?	.... No. Could I leave a message?
d Could I speak to Paul, please?	.... Yes. My number is 669 3241.
e Would you like to come to a party?	.... I'll see if he's in.
f I'm afraid she's busy at the moment.	.... My name's Gillian. Gillian Bond.
g Can I get her to call you back?	.... Yes, that would be great. Thanks.

3   **What would you say on the telephone in the following situations? Write sentences.**

Example
You want to know when you can call back.
When can I call back?

You want:

a   to speak to Kate James. ....

b   to cancel a meeting. ....

c   Janet to call you back. ....

d   Liam to ask Janet to call you back. ....

e   to know when the Manager will be back. ....

f   to ask a friend out to dinner. ....

4   **Match the verbs with appropriate nouns.**

a barbecue   *leave*   have   a message

watch

come   listen to   an appointment   give

make   do

a match   to dinner

a ring   go   play

music

the housework   football   swimming

5   **Complete the sentences. Then match the sentences on the left with a correct response on the right.**

1   There's a good film on at the
    Ritzy. (you / like / come / tonight)?

    ....

.... No, thanks. I (not like) talking
to people I don't know.

....

2   (you / like) go to the match this
    afternoon? I've got two tickets.

    ....

.... Sorry, I can't. (work / overtime.
/ tomorrow?)

....

3   (have to / get together) sometime.

    ....

.... Thanks, but I (not like)
watching sport.

....

4   (you / fancy / go) to a party?

    ....

.... Thanks, (be /nice).

....

5   (we / have / barbecue / Sunday).
    (you / like / come)?

    ....

.... Yes, (love to).

6 Write invitations for the social programme below.

My Social Week

Play   Tuesday night
Football match   Wednesday night
Jazz concert   Thursday night
Dinner   Friday night
Club   Saturday night
Walk in the park   Sunday afternoon
Cinema   Sunday night

Example

Would you like to go to a jazz concert on Thursday night? (or) Do you like listening to jazz? There's a concert on Thursday night.

a ....

b ....

c ....

d ....

e ....

f ....

7 Write about your plans for Friday, Saturday and Sunday like this.

I'm going to a business meeting on Friday morning. I'm having lunch with three people at one o' clock. On Friday evening, I'm going to a concert with an old friend from school.

....

....

....

....

....

....

8 Read the text about using a public telephone in Britain. Then answer the questions. Use a dictionary to help you if necessary.

Payphones

Public payphones (phones you put money in to make calls) can often be found in the streets in call-boxes and also in public buildings such as large shops. You'll find pictures and instructions near the phone to help you.

There are two main kinds of payphone. The first kind takes coins. Some coin-operated payphones take 10p, 20p and 50p coins; others take £1 coins too. To use these payphones you pick the phone up, put some money in, and then dial the number. These payphones will only return coins that aren't used at all, but they also have a 'next call' button, which you'll see when you pick up the phone. If you have money left to use in the machine after making a call, you can press this button and make another call using the remaining money. For example, if you put in a 50p coin and make a 30p call, you'll get no change, but you can press the button and use the remaining 20p for another call.

Cardphones take special cards instead of money. The cards are sold at post offices and in many shops; look for the green Phonecard sign. Some Cardphones at airports and large train stations also accept credit cards.

Emergency (999) calls: by dialling the emergency number – 999 – you can call the police, fire or ambulance services, and sometimes other emergency services too. These calls are free, even from payphones, but they should only be made when help is needed urgently. You'll find instructions by payphones and in the Phone Book.

a How can you pay for a public telephone call?

....

b Where can you usually find public phones in Britain?

....

c What money do you need to use a Cardphone?

....

d You see a terrible car accident in the street in London. What number do you dial?

....

e How much does this phone call cost?

....

What do you usually use the telephone for?

....

9 Rewrite the sentences. Use the words in brackets.

Example
Could you ask him to give me a ring? (call me)
Could you ask him to call me?

a Do you want to see a film? (Would / like)

....

b She's working late tomorrow. (overtime)

....

c Please tell her my number is 8472. (can / ring)

....

d We'll have to get together sometime. (one of these days)

....

e Are you free on Saturday? (do / anything)

....

10 Translate these sentences into your language. Use a dictionary or work with someone who speaks your language.

a Can you call back?

....

b Could you ask her to give me a call?

....

c I'll see that he gets the message.

....

d Hold the line please. The number's engaged.

....

e We'll have to get together sometime.

....

f Why not come over on Saturday evening?

....

Changes 1 Wordlist

In the words and expressions listed below, only primary stress and syllabic stress are marked. The figures following the phonemic transcription refer to the unit in which the word first appears.

a bit more /ə bɪt'mɔː/ 9
a lot /ə 'lɒt/ 4
about /ə'baʊt/ 3
accident /'æksɪdənt/ 10
accountant /ə'kaʊntənt/ 2
actor /'æktə/ 1
actress /'æktrəs/ 3
address /ə'dres/ 2
advice /əd'vaɪs/ 9
aerobics /eə'rəʊbɪks/ 1
aeroplane /'eərəpleɪn/ 10
after /'ɑːftə/ 3
afternoon /ɑːftə'nuːn/
again /ə'gen/ 9
airline /'eəlaɪn/ 10
airport /'eəpɔːt/ 8
alone /ə'ləʊn/ 11
always /'ɔːlweɪz/ 6
American /ə'merɪkən/ 1
and /ənd, ən, n̩/ 1
animal /'ænɪməl/ 15
ankle /'æŋkl̩/ 12
answer /'ɑːnsə/ 2
anyone /'eniwʌn/ 9
anything /'eniθɪŋ/ 10
apple /'æpl̩/ 13
appointment /ə'pɔɪntmənt/ 10
architect /'ɑːkɪtekt/ 1
architecture /'ɑːkɪtektʃə/ 11
area /'eərɪə/ 14
Argentina /ɑːdʒən'tiːnə/ 1
Argentinian /ɑːdʒən'tɪnɪən/ 1
arm /ɑːm/ 12
around /ə'raʊnd/ 7
arrive /ə'raɪv/ 7
art /ɑːt/ 11
art gallery /'ɑːt gælərɪ/ 8
as ... as /əz ... əz/ 14
as well /əz 'wel/ 6
ask /ɑːsk/ 10
aspirin /'æsprɪn/ 12
astrology /ə'strɒlədʒɪ/ 2
at /æt, ət/ 2
aunt /ɑːnt/ 5
Australia /ɒ'streɪlɪə/ 1

Australian /ɒ'streɪlɪən/ 1
Austria /'ɒstrɪə/ 1
Austrian /'ɒstrɪən/ 1
autumn /'ɔːtəm/ 11
awful /'ɔːfl̩/ 7
back /bæk/ 12
backache /'bækeɪk/ 12
bad /bæd/ 2
bag /bæg/ 3
balcony /'bælkənɪ/ 8
bald /bɔːld/ 9
ballet /'bæleɪ/ 15
banana /bə'nɑːnə/ 13
band /bænd/ 4
bank /bæŋk/ 2
bank account /'bæŋk əkaʊnt/ 9
bank manager /'bæŋk mænɪdʒə/ 1
bar /bɑː/ 2
barbecue /'bɑːbɪkjuː/ 15
baseball /'beɪsbɔːl/ 6
be /biː, bɪ/ 1
beach /biːtʃ/ 11
beans /biːnz/ 13
beard /bɪəd/ 5
beautiful /'bjuːtɪfl̩/ 11
bed /bed/ 6
bedroom /'bedrʊm/ 8
beef /biːf/ 13
beginning /bɪ'gɪnɪŋ/ 14
behind /bɪ'haɪnd/ 8
Belgian /'beldʒən/ 1
Belgium /'beldʒəm/ 1
belt /belt/ 3
between /bɪ'twiːn/ 8
bicycle /'baɪsɪkl̩/ 3
big /bɪg/ 8
black /blæk/ 9
blond(e) /blɒnd/ 9
blue /bluː/ 9
boat /bəʊt/ 11
book /bʊk/ 2
bookshop /'bʊk ʃɒp/ 2
boring /'bɔːrɪŋ/ 11
borrow /'bɒrəʊ/ 8

bottle /'bɒtl̩/ 12
bouncer /'baʊnsə/ 2
box /bɒks/ 12
bracelet /'breɪslət/ 3
Brazilian /brə'zɪlɪən/ 1
bread /bred/ 13
breakfast /'brekfəst/ 6
bridge /brɪdʒ/ 6
briefcase /'briːfkeɪs/ 3
bring /brɪŋ/ 10
Britain /'brɪtn̩/ 1
British /'brɪtɪʃ/ 1
brother /'brʌðə/ 5
brother-in-law /'brʌðərɪnlɔː/ 5
brown /braʊn/ 9
brush /brʌʃ/ 9
building /'bɪldɪŋ/ 11
burn /bɜːn/ 12
bus /bʌs/ 2
bus station /'bʌs steɪʃn̩/ 8
busiest /'bɪzɪəst/ 6
busy /'bɪzɪ/ 5
but /bʌt, bət/ 4
butcher's /'bʊtʃəz/ 8
butter /'bʌtə/ 14
cafe /'kæfeɪ/ 8
cake /keɪk/ 8
calculator /'kælkjəleɪtə/ 3
call /kɔːl/ 10
call back /kɔːl 'bæk/ 15
camera /'kæmrə/ 2
can /kæn, kən/ 1
Canada /'kænədə/ 12
Canadian /kə'neɪdɪən/ 1
canal /kə'næl̩/ 11
cancel /'kænsl̩/ 15
car /kɑː/ 3
carrot /'kærət/ 13
cashier /kæ'ʃɪə/ 2
cat /kæt/ 14
catch /kætʃ/ 6
catch cold /kætʃ 'kəʊld/ 12
CD player /siː'diː pleɪə/ 3
centre /'sentə/ 8
ceramics /sə'ræmɪks/ 4

certainly /'sɜːtnlɪ/ 12
chat show /'tʃæt ʃəʊ/ 4
cheap /tʃiːp/ 7
check in /tʃek'ɪn/ 10
chef /ʃef/ 2
chemist's /'kemɪsts/ 8
chest /tʃest/ 12
chicken /'tʃɪkɪn/ 3
chicken stock /tʃɪkɪn 'stɒk/ 12
children /'tʃɪldrən/ 5
Chile /'tʃɪlɪ/ 1
Chilean /'tʃɪlɪən/ 1
chin /tʃɪn/ 12
China /'tʃaɪnə/ 1
Chinese /tʃaɪ'niːz/ 1
chop up /tʃɒp 'ʌp/ 12
cinema /'sɪnəmə/ 3
class /klɑːs/ 1
classical music /klæsɪkl 'mjuːzɪk/ 4
classmate /'klɑːsmeɪt/ 1
clean /kliːn/ 11
cleaner /'kliːnə/ 2
clerk /klɑːk/ 1
clever /'klevə/ 14
cliff /klɪf/ 14
climate /'klaɪmət/ 11
coffee /'kɒfɪ/ 6
cold /kəʊld/ 11
colour /'kʌlə/ 3
come /kʌm/ 1
come round /kʌm 'raʊnd/ 6
company director /kʌmpənɪ dɪ'rektə/ 1
computer /kəm'pjuːtə/ 4
computer business /kəm'pjuːtə bɪznɪs/ 5
concert /'kɒnsət/ 4
continent /'kɒntɪnənt/ 14
convenient /kən'viːnɪənt/ 8
cough /kɒf/ 12
could /kʊd, kəd/ 12
counter /'kaʊntə/ 10
country /'kʌntrɪ/ 1
country music /'kʌntrɪ mjuːzɪk/ 4
countryside /'kʌntrɪsaɪd/ 11
cousin /'kʌzn̩/ 5
cream /kriːm/ 12
cross /krɒs/ 11
continent /'kɒntɪnənt/ 14
crowded /'kraʊdɪd/ 10
cup /kʌp/ 12
curly /'kɜːlɪ/ 9
customer /'kʌstəmə/ 3
cut /kʌt/ 12

cycle /'saɪkl̩/ 6
cycling /'saɪklɪŋ/ 6
Cyprus /'saɪprəs/ 10
dance /dɑːns/ 9
dance music /'dɑːns mjuːzɪk/ 4
dancing /'dɑːnsɪŋ/ 6
dangerous /'deɪndʒərəs/ 11
dark blue /dɑːk 'bluː/ 9
daughter /'dɔːtə/ 5
day off /deɪ 'ɒf/ 6
dead /ded/ 5
decide /dɪ'saɪd/ 13
delicious /dɪ'lɪʃəs/ 13
dentist /'dentɪst/ 12
deodorant /dɪ'əʊdərənt/ 12
department store /dɪ'pɑːtmənt stɔː/ 2
depend /dɪ'pend/ 6
desert /'dezət/ 14
dessert /dɪ'zɜːt/ 13
dictionary /'dɪkʃnrɪ/ 15
die /daɪ/ 7
dinner /'dɪnə/ 3
dirty /'dɜːtɪ/ 11
disagree /dɪsə'griː/ 14
disaster /dɪ'zɑːstə/ 10
dishwasher /'dɪʃwɒʃə/ 3
display /dɪ'spleɪ/ 4
DJ /diː 'dʒeɪ/ 2
do /duː, dʊ, də/ 2
doctor /'dɒktə/ 1
documentary /dɒkjə'mentrɪ/ 4
door /dɔː/ 9
drama /'drɑːmə/ 5
dreadful /'dredfl̩/ 12
dress /dres/ 3
dressing /'dresɪŋ/ 13
drink /drɪŋk/ 7
drive /draɪv/ 6
dry /draɪ/ 8
Dutch /dʌtʃ/ 1
each /iːtʃ/ 3
ear /ɪə/ 12
early /'ɜːlɪ/ 6
earrings /'ɪərɪŋz/ 7
economics /ekə'nɒmɪks/ 9
Egypt /'iːdʒɪpt/ 1
Egyptian /ɪ'dʒɪpʃn̩/ 1
eight /eɪt/ 2
eighty /'eɪtɪ/ 2
elbow /'elbəʊ/ 12
eleven /ɪ'levn̩/ 2
embassy /'embəsɪ/ 10
energy /'enədʒɪ/ 12
engineer /endʒɪ'nɪə/ 1
engineering /endʒɪ'nɪərɪŋ/ 2

England /'ɪŋglənd/ 1
English /'ɪŋglɪʃ/ 1
entertainment /entə'teɪnmənt/ 4
equipment /ɪ'kwɪpmənt/ 3
evening /'iːvnɪŋ/ 2
ever /'evə/ 6
every day /evrɪ 'deɪ/ 6
everybody /'evrɪbɒdɪ/ 11
everywhere /'evrɪweə/ 2
excellent /veksələnt/ 11
exciting /ɪk'saɪtɪŋ/ 11
exercise /'eksəsaɪz/ 6
exhibition /eksɪ'bɪʃn̩/ 4
expenses /ɪk'spensɪz/ 3
expensive /ɪk'spensɪv/ 11
explain /ɪk'spleɪn/ 10
eye /aɪ/ 12
face /feɪs/ 12
fairly /'feəlɪ/ 8
family /'fæmlɪ/ 5
fantastic /fæn'tæstɪk/ 7
farming /'fɑːmɪŋ/ 14
fascinating /'fæsɪneɪtɪŋ/ 11
fashion /'fæʃn̩/ 9
fashion business /'fæʃn̩ bɪznɪs/ 5
father /'fɑːðə/ 5
favourite /'feɪvrɪt/ 4
feel /fiːl/ 7
fever /'fiːvə/ 12
few /fjuː/ 10
field /fiːld/ 14
fifteen /fɪf'tiːn/ 2
fifty /'fɪftɪ/ 2
Filipino /fɪlɪ'piːnəʊ/ 1
fill in /fɪl 'ɪn/ 10
film /fɪlm/ 1
film star /'fɪlm stɑː/ 4
finally /'faɪnlɪ/ 10
financial /faɪ'nænʃl̩/ 9
finger /'fɪŋgə/ 12
fireworks /'faɪəwɜːks/ 4
first /fɜːst/ 1
fit /fɪt/ 6
five /faɪv/ 2
flat /flæt/ 8
flight /flaɪt/ 7
flight attendant /'flaɪt ətendənt/ 2
flour /flaʊə/ 13
flu /fluː/ 12
folder /'fəʊldə/ 3
folk music /'fəʊk mjuːzɪk/ 4
food /fuːd/ 2
foot /fʊt/ 12
football /'fʊtbɔːl/ 6
football match /'fʊtbɔːl mætʃ/ 4

footballer /'fʊtbɔːlə/ 1
for /fɔː, fə/ 2
foreign /'fɒrɪn/ 1
fork /fɔːk/ 13
form /fɔːm/ 10
forty /'fɔːtɪ/ 2
four /fɔː/ 2
fourteen /fɔː'tiːn/ 2
France /frɑːns/ 1
free /friː/ 1
French /frentʃ/ 1
French fries /'frentʃ fraɪz/ 13
Friday /'fraɪdɪ/ 1
friendly /'frendlɪ/ 13
from /frɒm, frəm/ 1
fruit /fruːt/ 13
fruit juice /'fruːt dʒuːs/
full /fʊl/ 1
full-time /fʊl'taɪm/ 2
game /geɪm/ 8
game show /'geɪm ʃəʊ/ 4
garage / 'gærɑːʒ/ 2
garden /'gɑːdn̩/ 8
garlic /'gɑːlɪk/ 12
German /'dʒɜːmən/ 1
Germany /'dʒɜːmənɪ/ 1
get /get/ 6
get to /'get tʊ, tə/ 7
give /gɪv/ 7
glass /glɑːs/ 13
glasses /'glɑːsɪz/ 3
go /gəʊ/ 5
go for a run /gʊə fər ə 'rʌn/ 6
go home /gʊə 'həʊm/ 6
go out /gʊə 'aʊt/ 7
gold /gəʊld/ 14
golf /gɒlf/ 6
gondola /'gɒndələ/ 11
grain /greɪn/ 13
grandfather /'grænfɑːðə/ 5
grandmother /'grænmʌðə/ 5
grandparent /'grænpeərənt/ 5
greasy /'griːsɪ/ 13
great /greɪt/ 2
Greece /griːs/ 1
Greek /griːk/ 1
green /griːn/ 3
grey /greɪ/ 9
groceries /'grəʊsərɪz/ 8
group /gruːp/ 4
grow /grəʊ/ 14
guide /gaɪd/ 2
hair /heə/ 9
hairdresser's /'heədresəz/ 8
hairspray /'heəspreɪ/ 12
half hour /hɑːf 'aʊə/ 12

hand /hænd/ 12
happen /'hæpən/ 10
harbour /'hɑːbə/ 11
hard /hɑːd/ 9
hardware shop /'hɑːdweə ʃɒp/ 8
have /hæv, həv, əv/ 2
have time /hæv 'taɪm/ 7
head /hed/ 12
headphones /'hedfəʊnz/ 3
health /helθ/ 12
healthy /'helθɪ/ 14
heavy /'hevɪ/ 12
heavy metal /hevɪ 'metl̩/ 4
height /haɪt/ 9
hello /hə'ləʊ/ 1
here /hɪə/ 1
hi /haɪ/ 1
hiccups /'hɪkʌps/ 12
high /haɪ/ 14
hike /haɪk/ 6
hiking /'haɪkɪŋ/ 6
hill /hɪl/ 14
hip /hɪp/ 12
hire /haɪə/ 7
history /'hɪstrɪ/ 11
hitch /hɪtʃ/ 10
hockey /'hɒkɪ/ 15
Holland /'hɒlənd/ 1
home town /həʊm 'taʊn/ 11
homework /'həʊmwɜːk/ 10
horror film /'hɒrə fɪlm/ 4
horse /hɔːs/ 14
hospital /'hɒspɪtl̩/ 2
hot /hɒt/ 11
hotel /həʊ'tel/ 2
house /haʊs/ 8
house music /'haʊs mjuːzɪk/ 4
housework /'haʊswɜːk/ 6
how /haʊ/ 5
hundred /'hʌndrəd/ 2
Hungarian /hʌŋ'geərɪən/ 1
Hungary /'hʌŋgərɪ/ 1
hurt /hɜːt/ 12
husband /'hʌzbənd/ 5
ice /aɪs/ 12
ice cream /aɪs 'kriːm/ 13
important /ɪm'pɔːtənt/ 10
in /ɪn/ 1
India /'ɪndɪə/ 10
Indian /'ɪndɪən/ 10
indigestion /ɪndɪ'dʒestʃən/ 12
insect bite /'ɪnsekt baɪt/ 12
insomnia /ɪn'sɒmnɪə/ 12
interesting /'ɪntrəstɪŋ/ 5
into /'ɪntuː, 'ɪntʊ, 'ɪntə/ 8
invite /ɪn'vaɪt/ 7

Iran /ɪ'rɑːn/ 10
Ireland /'aɪələnd/ 1
Irish /'aɪrɪʃ/ 1
island /'aɪlənd/ 7
it /ɪt/ 3
Italian /ɪ'tælɪən/ 1
Italy /'ɪtlɪ/ 1
jacket /'dʒækɪt/ 3
Japan /dʒə'pæn/ 1
Japanese /dʒæpə'niːz/ 1
jar /dʒɑː/ 12
jazz /dʒæz/ 4
jeans /dʒiːnz/ 3
job /dʒɒb/ 1
jog /dʒɒg/ 6
Jordan /'dʒɔːdn̩/ 1
Jordanian /dʒɔː'deɪnɪən/ 1
jumper /'dʒʌmpə/ 9
just /dʒʌst, djəst/ 10
Kenya /'kenjə/ 1
Kenyan /'kenjən/ 1
kilometre /'kɪlɒmɪtə/ 14
kitchen /'kɪtʃɪn/ 8
knee /niː/ 12
know /nəʊ/ 4
Korea /kə'rɪə/ 1
Korean /kə'rɪən/ 1
Kuwait /kʊ'weɪt/ 1
Kuwaiti /kʊ'weɪtɪ/ 1
lake /leɪk/ 14
language /'læŋgwɪdʒ/ 1
large /lɑːdʒ/ 14
last /lɑːst/ 1
late /leɪt/ 6
launderette /lɔːn'dret/ 8
lawn /lɔːn/ 9
lawyer /'lɔːjə/ 1
lazy /'leɪzɪ/ 6
leather /'leðə/ 7
leave /liːv/ 7
lecture /'lektʃə/ 4
leg /leg/ 12
less /les/ 14
lesson /'lesn̩/ 7
letter /'letə/ 8
library /'laɪbrɪ/ 8
lie down /laɪ 'daʊn/ 12
lift /lɪft/ 12
light blue /laɪt 'bluː/ 9
like /laɪk/ 4
liquid /'lɪkwɪd/ 12
listen to /'lɪsn̩ tʊ, tə/ 7
literature /'lɪtrətʃə/ 15
litre /'liːtə/ 3
living room /'lɪvɪŋ rʊm/ 8
long /lɒŋ/ 9

look /lʊk/ 3
look like /'lʊk laɪk/ 9
lose /luːz/ 7
lots of /'lɒts əv/ 11
love /lʌv/ 2
luggage /'lʌgɪdʒ/ 10
lunch /lʌntʃ/ 6
man /mæn/ 5
manage /'mænɪdʒ/ 5
manager /'mænɪdʒə/ 2
married /'mærɪd/ 5
marry /'mærɪ/ 7
match /mætʃ/ 15
meal /miːl/ 2
meat /miːt/ 13
mechanic /mɪ'kænɪk/ 2
medicine /'medsən/ 8
medium /'miːdɪəm/ 9
meet /miːt/ 6
meeting /'miːtɪŋ/ 15
menu /'menjuː/ 13
message /'mesɪdʒ/ 15
Mexican /'meksɪkən/ 1
Mexico /'meksɪkəʊ/ 1
midday /mɪd'deɪ/ 6
midnight /'mɪdnaɪt/ 10
mile /maɪl/ 14
milk /mɪlk/ 13
Miss /mɪs/ 1
miss /mɪs/ 11
missing /'mɪsɪŋ/ 9
model /'mɒdl̩/ 3
modern /'mɒdn̩/ 11
Monday /'mʌndɪ/ 1
more /mɔː/ 14
morning /'mɔːnɪŋ/ 10
mother /'mʌðə/ 5
motorbike /'məʊtəbaɪk/ 3
motorway /'məʊtəweɪ/ 14
mountain /'maʊntɪn/ 11
moustache /mə'staːʃ/ 9
mouth /maʊθ/ 3
move /muːv/ 8
move in /muːv 'ɪn/ 8
mow /məʊ/ 9
Mr /'mɪstə/ 1
Mrs /'mɪsɪz/ 1
Ms /mɪz, məz/ 1
much /mʌtʃ/ 14
mum /mʌm/ 7
muscle /'mʌsl̩/ 12
museum /mjuː'zɪəm/ 11
music /'mjuːzɪk/ 4
musical /'mjuːzɪkl̩/ 15
name /neɪm/ 1
nationality /næʃə'nælətɪ/ 1

nature /'neɪtʃə/ 4
near /nɪə/ 8
nearby /nɪə'baɪ/ 8
nearly /'nɪəlɪ/ 14
neck /nek/ 12
necklace /'nekləs/ 3
neighbour /'neɪbə/ 8
neighbourhood /'neɪbəhʊd/ 8
Nepal /nɪ'pɔːl/ 10
nephew /'nefjuː/ 5
Netherlands /'neðələndz/ 1
never /'nevə/ 6
New Zealand /njuː'ziːlənd/ 1
New Zealander /njuː 'ziːləndə/ 1
new /njuː/ 3
news /njuːz/ 4
newsagent /'njuːzeɪdʒənt/ 8
next /nekst/ 10
next to /'nekst tʊ, tə/ 8
niece /niːs/ 5
Nigeria /naɪ'dʒɪərɪə/ 1
Nigerian /naɪ'dʒɪərɪən/ 1
night /naɪt/ 6
night club /'naɪt klʌb/ 2
nine /naɪn/ 2
ninety /'naɪntɪ/ 2
noisy /'nɔɪzɪ/ 11
northern /'nɔːðn̩/ 14
nose /nəʊz/ 12
nothing /'nʌθɪŋ/ 3
now /naʊ/ 1
number /'nʌmbə/ 1
ocean /'əʊʃn̩/ 14
of /ɒv, əv/ 3
office /'ɒfɪs/ 2
often /'ɒfn̩/ 6
ointment /'ɔɪntmənt/ 12
on /ɒn/ 2
on the corner of /ɒn ðə 'kɔːnər əv/ 8
once /wʌns/ 6
one /wʌn/ 2
only /'əʊnlɪ/ 3
opera /'ɒprə/ 11
opera singer /'ɒprə sɪŋə/ 1
opposite /'ɒpəzɪt/ 8
orange /'ɒrɪndʒ/ 9
orange juice /'ɒrɪndʒ dʒuːs/ 13
order /'ɔːdə/ 13
overcooked /əʊvə'kʊkt/ 13
overtime /'əʊvətaɪm/ 15
own /əʊn/ 10
pack /pæk/ 12
package holiday /pækɪdʒ 'hɒlɪdɪ/ 7
pain /peɪn/ 12

painful /'peɪnfl̩/ 12
parent /'peərənt/ 5
park /paːk/ 4
parking ticket /'paːkɪŋ tɪkɪt/ 10
part-time /paːt 'taɪm/ 2
party /'paːtɪ/ 7
passenger /'pæsɪndʒə/ 2
passport /'paːspɔːt/ 10
passport number /'paːspɔːt nʌmbə/ 2
pasta /'pæstə/ 13
pastille /'pæstl̩/ 12
path /paːθ/ 14
patient /'peɪʃnt/ 2
pay /peɪ/ 8
pencil /'pensl̩/ 3
people /'piːpl̩/ 2
perhaps /pə'hæps/ 13
person /'pɜːsn̩/ 9
Peru /pə'ruː/ 1
Peruvian /pə'ruːvɪən/ 1
petrol /'petrəl/ 3
petrol station /'petrəl steɪʃn̩/ 8
Philippines /'fɪlɪpiːnz/ 1
phone /fəʊn/ 2
phone box /'fəʊn bɒks/ 8
photo /'fəʊtəʊ/ 7
photographer /fə'tɒgrəfə/ 2
picnic /'pɪknɪk/ 15
pie /paɪ/ 13
pink /pɪŋk/ 9
place /pleɪs/ 11
plant /plaːnt/ 14
plate /pleɪt/ 13
play /pleɪ/ 4
Poland /'pəʊlənd/ 1
police station /pə'liːs steɪʃn̩/ 10
polite /pə'laɪt/ 13
pop /pɒp/ 4
populated /'pɒpjəleɪtɪd/ 14
Portugese /pɔːtʃə'giːz/ 1
post /pəʊst/ 8
post box /'pəʊs bɒks/ 8
post office /'pəʊst ɒfɪs/ 5
postcard /'pəʊs kaːd/ 7
potato /pə'teɪtəʊ/ 13
prefer /prɪ'fɜː/ 4
prepare /prɪ'peə/ 2
present /'prezn̩t/ 7
price /praɪs/ 3
public toilet /pʌblɪk 'tɔɪlət/ 8
public transport /pʌblɪk 'trænspɔːt/ 8
publishing company /'pʌblɪʃɪŋ kʌmpənɪ/ 2
purple /'pɜːpl̩/ 9

quick /kwɪk/ 13
quiet /ˈkwaɪət/ 8
quite /kwaɪt/ 9
radio /ˈreɪdɪəʊ/ 4
rap /ræp/ 4
rarely /ˈreəlɪ/ 6
rather /ˈrɑːðə/ 6
read /riːd/ 7
reasonable /ˈriːznəbl̩/ 13
receptionist /rɪˈsepʃənɪst/ 1
recommend /rekəˈmend/ 13
red /red/ 9
reduction /rɪˈdʌkʃn̩/ 3
refrigerator /rɪˈfrɪdʒəreɪtə/ 3
reggae /ˈregeɪ/ 4
rent /rent/ 8
repair /rɪˈpeə/ 2
reporter /rɪˈpɔːtə/ 1
reservation /rezəˈveɪʃn/ 13
rest /rest/ 8
retired /rɪˈtaɪəd/ 5
return a call /rɪtɜːn ə ˈkɔːl/ 15
rice /raɪs/ 13
ride /raɪd/ 10
ring /rɪŋ/ 3
river /ˈrɪvə/ 11
rock /rɒk/ 4
round /raʊnd/ 10
rude /ruːd/ 13
run /rʌn/ 6
safe /seɪf/ 11
sail /seɪl/ 10
salad /ˈsæləd/ 13
sale /seɪl/ 3
sales assistant /ˈseɪlz əsɪstənt/ 2
sales representative /ˈseɪlz
    reprɪzentətɪv/ 1
salmon /ˈsæmən/ 13
salty /ˈsɒltɪ/ 13
sandwich /ˈsænwɪdʒ/ 13
Saturday /ˈsætədɪ/ 1
Saudi Arabia /saʊdɪ əˈreɪbɪə/ 1
Saudi Arabian /saʊdɪ əˈreɪbɪən/ 1
school /skuːl/ 2
school teacher /ˈskuːl tiːtʃə/ 2
science fiction /saɪəns ˈfɪkʃn̩/ 4
scientist /ˈsaɪəntɪst/ 2
seat /siːt/ 1
second /ˈsekənd/ 1
secretary /ˈsekrətrɪ/ 1
section /ˈsekʃn̩/ 2
see /siː/ 3
sell /sel/ 2
send /send/ 7
serve /sɜːv/ 2
seven /ˈsevn̩/ 2

seventy /ˈsevn̩tɪ/ 2
shampoo /ʃæmˈpuː/ 12
shark /ʃɑːk/ 7
shave /ʃeɪv/ 9
shaving cream /ˈʃeɪvɪŋ kriːm/ 12
shirt /ʃɜːt/ 3
shoe /ʃuː/ 3
shoe shop /ˈʃuː ʃɒp/ 8
shop /ʃɒp/ 2
shop assistant /ˈʃɒp əsɪstənt/ 2
shopping centre /ˈʃɒpɪŋ sentə/ 8
short /ʃɔːt/ 9
should /ʃʊd, ʃəd/ 11
shrine /ʃraɪn/ 11
sick /sɪk/ 12
singer /ˈsɪŋə/ 4
single /ˈsɪŋgl̩/ 5
sister-in-law /ˈsɪstərɪnlɔː/ 5
sit /sɪt/ 9
six /sɪks/ 2
sixty /ˈsɪkstɪ/ 2
skiing /ˈskiːɪŋ/ 6
skirt /skɜːt/ 3
sleep /sliːp/ 6
slow /sləʊ/ 13
slow down /sləʊ ˈdaʊn/ 10
small /smɔːl/ 11
snow /snəʊ/ 14
so /səʊ/ 6
soap /səʊp/ 12
soaps /səʊps/ 4
somebody /ˈsʌmbədɪ/ 9
someone /ˈsʌmwʌn/ 9
something /ˈsʌmθɪŋ/ 12
sometimes /ˈsʌmtaɪmz/ 6
son /sʌn/ 5
sore /sɔː/ 12
sore throat /sɔː ˈθrəʊt/ 12
soup /suːp/ 13
Spain /speɪn/ 1
Spanish /ˈspænɪʃ/ 1
speak /spiːk/ 7
speeding ticket /ˈspiːdɪŋ tɪkɪt/ 10
spend /spend/ 3
spoon /spuːn/ 13
sport /spɔːt/ 4
sports car /ˈspɔːts kɑː/ 10
spring /sprɪŋ/ 11
squash /skwɒʃ/ 6
squash racquet /ˈskwɒʃ rækɪt/ 3
stamp /stæmp/ 8
stand /stænd/ 9
start /stɑːt/ 4
stay in /steɪ ˈɪn/ 6
steak /steɪk/ 13
stick /stɪk/ 12

stiff neck /stɪf ˈnek/ 12
still /stɪl/ 3
stomach /ˈstʌmək/ 12
straight /streɪt/ 6
strange /streɪndʒ/ 10
strawberry /ˈstrɔːbərɪ/ 13
stream /striːm/ 14
stress /stres/ 12
student /ˈstjuːdn̩t/ 1
study / ˈstʌdɪ/ 7
summer /ˈsʌmə/ 10
sunburn /ˈsʌnbɜːn/ 12
Sunday /ˈsʌndɪ/ 1
sunny /ˈsʌnɪ/ 11
supermarket /ˈsuːpəmɑːkɪt/ 8
supervisor /ˈsuːpəvaɪzə/ 1
suppose /səˈpəʊz/ 11
sure /ʃɔː/ 13
Sweden /ˈswiːdn̩/ 1
Swedish /ˈswiːdɪʃ/ 1
swimming /ˈswɪmɪŋ/ 6
Swiss /swɪs/ 1
Switzerland /ˈswɪtsələnd/ 1
T-shirt /ˈtiː ʃɜːt/ 9
tablet /ˈtæblɪt/ 12
Taiwan /taɪˈwɑːn/ 1
Taiwanese /taɪwənˈiːz/ 1
take /teɪk/ 2
take off /teɪk ˈɒf/ 10
talk /tɔːk/ 9
tall /tɔːl/ 9
tank /tæŋk/ 12
tasteless /ˈteɪstləs/ 3
tasty /ˈteɪstɪ/ 13
tea /tiː/ 6
teach /tiːtʃ/ 2
teacher /ˈtiːtʃə/ 1
technician /tekˈnɪʃn̩/ 10
tell /tel/ 15
temperature /ˈtemprətʃə/ 12
temple /ˈtempl̩/ 7
ten /ten/ 2
tender /ˈtendə/ 13
tennis /ˈtenɪs/ 6
tennis player /ˈtenɪs pleɪə/ 1
terrible /ˈterɪbl̩/ 9
than /ðæn, ðən/ 14
that /ðæt, ðət/ 2
theatre /ˈθɪətə/ 4
then /ðen/ 10
these /ðiːz/ 2
thing /θɪŋ/ 10
think /θɪŋk/ 2
thirteen /θɜːˈtiːn/ 2
thirties /ˈθɜːtɪz/ 9
thirty /ˈθɜːtɪ/ 2

thousand /'θaʊzn̩d/ 2
three /θriː/ 2
thriller /'θrɪlə/ 4
through /θruː/ 10
Thursday /'θɜːzdɪ/ 1
ticket /'tɪkɪt/ 3
tie /taɪ/ 3
till /tɪl/ 4
times /taɪmz/ 6
tissue /'tɪʃuː/
to /tuː, tʊ, tə/ 1
today /tə'deɪ/ 2
toe /təʊ/ 12
tomorrow /tə'mɒrəʊ/ 2
tonight /tə'naɪt/ 2
too /tuː/ 1
tooth /tuːθ/ 12
toothache /'tuːθeɪk/ 12
toothpaste /'tuːθpeɪst/ 12
touch of flu /tʌtʃ əv 'fluː/ 12
tough /tʌf/ 13
tour /tɔː/ 2
tourist /'tɔːrɪst/ 2
tournament /'tɔːnəmənt/ 15
town /taʊn/ 14
town centre /taʊn 'sentə/ 8
track /træk/ 14
traffic /'træfɪk/ 0
train driver /'treɪn draɪvə/ 2
transport /'trænspɔːt/ 10
travel /'trævl̩/ 4
travel agent /'trævl̩ eɪdʒənt/ 8
tree /triː/ 12
trip /trɪp/ 7
trousers /'traʊzəz/ 3
try /traɪ/ 8
tube /tjuːb/ 12
Tuesday /'tjuːzdɪ/ 1

Turkey /'tɜːkɪ/ 1
turkey /'tɜːkɪ/ 13
Turkish /'tɜːkɪʃ/ 1
TV /tiː 'viː/ 2
twelve /twelv/ 2
twenty /'twentɪ/ 2
twenty-one /twentɪ 'wʌn/ 2
twenty-two /twentɪ 'tuː/ 2
twice /twaɪs/ 6
two /tuː/ 2
typist /'taɪpɪst/ 1
UFO /juː ef 'əʊ/ 10
ugly /'ʌglɪ/ 11
umbrella /ʌm'brelə/ 11
uncle /'ʌnkl̩/ 5
undercooked /ʌndə'kʊkt/ 13
understand /ʌndə'stænd/ 7
unfriendly /ʌn'frendlɪ/ 13
United States /juːnaɪtɪd 'steɪts/ 1
unusual /ʌn'juːʒʊəl/ 10
Uruguay /'jʊərəgwaɪ/ 1
Uruguayan /jʊərə'gwaɪən/ 1
usually /'juːʒʊəlɪ/ 6
valley /'vælɪ/ 14
van /væn/ 10
vegetable /'vedʒtəbl̩/ 13
vehicle /'viːɪkl̩/ 10
very /'verɪ/ 6
very much /verɪ 'mʌtʃ/ 4
video /'vɪdɪəʊ/ 3
village /'vɪlɪdʒ/ 14
vitamin C /vɪtəmɪn 'siː/ 12
vitamin E /vɪtəmɪn 'iː/ 12
waiter /'weɪtə/ 2
walk /wɔːk/ 6
walk round /wɔːk 'raʊnd/ 7
want /wɒnt/ 4
war films /'wɔː fɪlmz/ 4

warm /wɔːm/ 11
wash /wɒʃ/ 8
watch /wɒtʃ/ 3
water /'wɔːtə/ 13
wear /weə/ 5
weather /'weðə/ 7
wedding /'wedɪŋ/
Wednesday /'wenzdɪ/ 1
week /wiːk/ 3
weekend /wiːk'end/ 1
westerns /'westənz/ 4
wet /wet/ 10
what /wɒt/ 1
when /wen/ 4
where /weə/ 1
white /waɪt/ 3
who /huː/ 2
whole /həʊl/ 12
wife /waɪf/ 5
window /'wɪndəʊ/ 9
winter /'wɪntə/ 11
with /wɪð/ 1
without /wɪð'aʊt/ 1
woman /'wʊmən/ 5
wood /wʊd,wəd/ 14
work /wɜːk/ 2
work out /wɜːk 'aʊt/ 6
world /wɜːld/ 10
worry /'wʌrɪ/ 10
would /wʊd, wəd/ 12
wrist /rɪst/ 12
write /raɪt/ 7
year /jɪə/ 6
yellow /'jeləʊ/ 3
yet /jet/ 10
yoga /'jəʊgə/ 1
yogurt /'jɒgət/ 13

Acknowledgements

The authors and publishers are grateful to Christine Lindop and Dominic Fisher for permission to reproduce copyright material from *Discover Britain*, Cambridge University Press on page 79.

The authors and publishers are grateful to the following illustrators and photographic sources:

Illustrators:
Kathy Baxendale: pp. 6, 52; David Downton: pp. 4, 6, 29, 46, 48, 55, 61, 67, 80; Annie Farrall: pp. 13, 15, 44, 65, 76; Sue Hillwood-Harris: pp. 7, 22, 30, 35, 50, 54, 60, 70; Conny Jude: pp. 5, 17, 28, 31, 34, 45, 47, 53, 62, 63, 64.

Photographers/Photographic sources:
Ace Photo Agency, p. 27 (centre right); Angloschool, p. 8; Barnabys Picture Library, pp. 23 (below), 32 (right), 36, 38 (below), 56 (above), 57 (above, below), 58, 71 (above); British Telecommunications plc, p. 17 (right); Camera Press, pp. 26 (above right) /photo Theodore Wood, 74 (below right); The J. Allan Cash Photolibrary, pp. 23 (above), 32 (left), 38 (above), 52, 56 (below), 71 (below), 74 (above, above centre left, below left), 79 (centre); Chrysler Jeep Imports UK, p. 51; © 1992 Comstock/Julian Nieman/SGC, p. 74 (above centre right); Art Directors Photo Library, p. 9 (below left); Greg Evans International, p. 68; Chris Fairclough Colour Library, pp. 10 (below right), 39 (left); Maggie Murray/Format Partners Photo Library, p. 57 (centre), Brenda Prince/Format, p. 9 (above right); Sally and Richard Greenhill, pp. 10 (above left), 14 (below), 25, 27 (above left), 59 (above centre), 78 (right), 79 (above); Dick Harding, p. 59 (below); Robert Harding Picture Library, pp. 49 (left), 75 (right); Hotpoint Limited, Peterborough, UK., p. 17 (above left); Peter Arkell/Impact Photos, p. 27 (centre left); Stan Laurel Prods/Hal Roach - MGM (Courtesy Kobal), p. 19 (above left), Paramount (Courtesy Kobal), p. 19 (below right), United Artists (Courtesy Kobal), p. 19 (above right), Universal (Courtesy Kobal), p. 19 (above centre, below left); Peter Lake, p. 16 (above, centre); Lloyds Bank, p. 27 (below left); Roger Hutchings/Network Photographers, p. 9 (above left), 78 (left); Crispin Hughes/Photofusion, p. 39 (centre right), Sally Lancaster/Photofusion, p. 59 (below centre); Pictor International, p. 66; Picturepoint-London, pp. 37 (right), 39 (right), 78 (centre); Graham Portlock, pp. 10 (above right), 11 (above, below), 14 (above), 79 (below); Rex Features Limited, p. 26 (below left); Sony Consumer Products Products UK Limited, p. 16 (below); Spectrum Colour Library, p. 37 (left), 74 (below centre); Tony Stone Images, pp. 27 (below right), 59 (above), 75 (left); Syndication International Limited, pp. 26 (above left), 26 (below right); Telegraph Colour Library, pp. 4, 49 (right); John Walmsley, p. 10 (below left); Whirlpool UK, p. 17 (below left); Janine Wiedel, pp. 9 (below right), 39 (cenrre left), 49 (centre).

Picture Research by Sandie Huskinson-Rolfe (PHOTOSEEKERS)

Design by Randell Harris